The Municipal Art Society of New York

MASNYC

# 10 Architectural Walks in Manhattan

# 10 Architectural Walks in Manhattan

# FRANCIS MORRONE AND
# MATTHEW A. POSTAL

## Photography by EDWARD A. TORAN

Foreword by KENT L. BARWICK

ROBIN LYNN, Editor

W. W. NORTON & COMPANY
NEW YORK AND LONDON

**Dedicated to Henry Hope Reed**

This book was made possible by a grant from
**Furthermore: a program of the J. M. Kaplan Fund.**

Pages 20–21, St. Paul's Chapel; 46–47, Park Row Building; 76–77, The High Line;
104–5, Appellate Division of the New York State Supreme Court; 128–29, General
Electric Building; 154–55, Main Concourse, Grand Central Terminal; 186–87, Plaza
at Seagram Building; 212–13, Window wall facing Columbus Circle; 240–41, Elm trees along the
Mall; 270–71, Hamilton Terrace; 296–97 Central Park Lake

For information about permission to reproduce selections from this book,
write to Permissions, W. W. Norton & Company, Inc.
500 Fifth Avenue, New York, NY 10110

For information about special discounts for bulk purchases, please contact
W. W. Norton Special Sales at specialsales@wwnorton.com or 800-233-4830

Manufacturing by KHL Printing
Book design by Abigail Sturges
Production manager: Leeann Graham

**Library of Congress Cataloging-in-Publication Data**
Morrone, Francis, 1958–
  The Municipal Art Society of New York : 10 architectural walks in
Manhattan / Francis Morrone and Matthew A. Postal ; foreword by Kent L.
Barwick ; photography by Edward A. Toran ; Robin Lynn, editor. — 1st ed.
      p. cm.
  Includes index.
  ISBN 978-0-393-73257-3 (pbk.)
  1. Architecture—New York (State)—New York—Tours. 2. Manhattan
(New York, N.Y.)—Buildings, structures, etc.—Tours. 3. Manhattan
(New York, N.Y.)—Tours. 4. New York (N.Y.)—Buildings, structures,
etc.—Tours. 5. New York (N.Y.)—Tours. I. Postal, Matthew A.
II. Toran, Edward A. III. Lynn, Robin. IV. Municipal Art Society of
New York. V. Title. VI. Title: 10 architectural walks in Manhattan.
  NA735.N5.M65 2009
  720.9747'1—dc22
                                        2008039520

W. W. Norton & Company, Inc.
500 Fifth Avenue, New York, N.Y. 10110
www.wwnorton.com

W. W. Norton & Company Ltd.
Castle House, 75/76 Wells Street, London W1T 3QT

0 9 8 7 6 5 4 3 2 1

# Contents

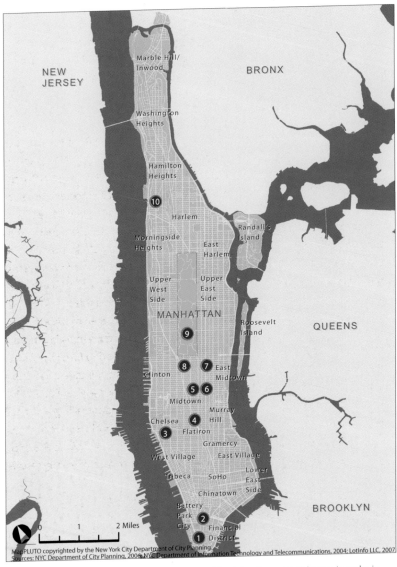

NEW
JERSEY

Marble Hill/
Inwood

BRONX

Washington
Heights

Hamilton
Heights

⑩

Harlem

Morningside
Heights

East
Harlem

Randall's
Island

Upper
West
Side

Upper
East
Side

MANHATTAN

Roosevelt
Island

QUEENS

⑨

⑧ ⑦ East
Midtown

Clinton

⑤ ⑥

Midtown

Murray
Hill

Chelsea ④

⑧ Flatiron

Gramercy

West Village

East Village

Tribeca

SoHo

Lower
East
Side

Chinatown

Battery
Park
City

②

Financial
District

①

BROOKLYN

0        1        2 Miles

MAS walks are offered in the financial district, in residential and commercial areas, in parks, in Grand Central Terminal, and in other vital neighborhoods throughout the five boroughs. The ten tours described in this book are highlighted on this map. From Wall Street to Harlem, they represent a sampler of popular MAS tours in Manhattan.

# Foreword

KENT L. BARWICK

On April 8, 1956, architectural historian Henry Hope Reed led what was not only the first Municipal Art Society of New York (MAS) walking tour but also probably New York's first architectural walking tour for the general public. It was so novel that the *New York Times* sent a reporter and a photographer to cover it. The *Times*'s reporter documented the bewildered looks and comments of passersby at the sight of thirty-eight individuals walking along the streets through a spring snowstorm, stopping to look at old buildings. The group was taken for bird-watchers or people in search of rooms to rent. In fact, the hardy tour-takers were part of a MAS effort to build a constituency that would support the preservation of the city's notable architecture.

Since the founding of MAS in 1893, the nonprofit, membership-based organization has fought for intelligent urban planning, design, and preservation through education, dialogue, and advocacy. By 1956, MAS had helped to foster the formation of the planning and art commissions and had influenced the city's urban design in large and small ways, from helping to defeat a plan for a bridge from Battery Park to Brooklyn to planting the city's first street trees. An enormous challenge lay ahead.

It's a truism that bad times are good for preservation. Money for new construction was in short supply during the Great Depression and World War II, but in the boom years of the 1950s New York's historic architecture was threatened as never before.

In addition to researching the strategies of other cities and the legal framework for protecting buildings, the board and members of MAS (there was no paid staff) joined forces with the Society of Architectural Historians to identify what was worth saving. The resulting index provided the basis for a 1955 exhibition, Monuments of Manhattan, which was curated by Henry Hope Reed and mounted at the University Club. It was a worthy exhibition, but it reached a limited audience: the members of the club and invited guests.

The next year, Reed and the painter E. Powis Jones found themselves serving together on the MAS Activities Committee. Recognizing that it was essential to broaden the preservation constituency, they proposed adapting a feature of Parisian Sundays, the "visites-conférences" (literally, visits-lectures), to New York. Unlike the clubs and private organizations where preservation events had previously taken place, the walking tours would be on the streets and open to all.

The MAS walking tours proved useful to preservation efforts in several ways. They made the case to a broad audience that the city's architecture was significant and worthy of preservation. The writer Brendan Gill reported on the first and subsequent tours for *The New Yorker*, remarking after one tour: "we saw, as if for the first time, buildings we have looked at all our life." Getting citizens to take the time to look, and to recognize the value of what they saw, was essential to building a preservation ethic. Clearly, the early tours provided newsworthy events for influential newspapers and magazines. Many who never took a MAS tour read about them, including the city's decision makers, who may also have realized that those taking two-hour walking tours in inclement weather were probable voters.

Reed later recalled that MAS president Harmon Goldstone said that the tours "were the single most important instrument in alerting New Yorkers to their landmarks." As New Yorkers came to appreciate the significance of the historic architecture around them, they knew that they didn't want it taken away.

New York City's 1965 Landmarks Law and the subsequent Landmarks Preservation Commission were preservation victories in which the MAS walking tour played a small but vital role.

Then as now, MAS tours were not confined to what was old. MAS advocates for excellence in contemporary architecture as well as historic preservation. In 1959, MAS asked architectural historian Ada Louise Huxtable to write a series of modernist walking tours, later published as a book by MAS and the Museum of Modern Art.

At the time of the first tour in 1956, Reed had already coauthored *American Skyline: The Growth and Form of Our Cities and Towns*. He went on to write many distinguished books on American classicism, including several on New York City buildings and parks. Huxtable became the *New York Times*'s first architecture critic in 1963, and in 1970 was the first architecture critic to win the Pulitzer Prize.

The walking tour in this book by Francis Morrone, "Of Farragut and Flatiron," looks at the same area that Reed, a friend and fellow classicist, focused on for his first MAS tour. Matthew A. Postal, who specializes in twentieth-century architecture and urbanism, wrote "When It Was New: Park Avenue," concentrat-

An MAS tour group next to Isamu Noguchi's *Cube*, 1973, on the plaza at 140 Broadway.

ing on the same area that inspired Huxtable's first walking tour. That many buildings Reed and Huxtable described remain standing is a tribute to their hard work and that of many other individuals and organizations.

Unlike a guided walking tour, this book has the advantage of being available whenever you wish to hit the streets—early in the morning, over a long lunch, or on a Sunday afternoon of your choosing. You will be following in the footsteps of celebrated and anonymous walkers who share the sidewalks—and their love of New York.

Built by Citibank in the mid-1970s, the Citigroup Center
incorporates a sunken outdoor plaza and multilevel atrium.

# Introduction

TAMARA COOMBS and ROBIN LYNN

Since its creation, the MAS walking tour program has grown from a semi-annual event to more than 200 tours a year. The architectural walking tour is no longer novel, but it remains an indispensable advocacy tool at MAS. There is no better way to appreciate an issue regarding a site, a building, or a neighborhood than to see what's at stake firsthand, in the company of an informed and engaging tour leader. The weekly MAS tour of Grand Central Terminal began more than thirty years ago as part of the campaign to save and restore the Beaux-Arts masterpiece. Today, Grand Central is a premier tourist destination, and our continuing Wednesday tours celebrate the preservation and economic rejuvenation of the terminal. These days, most MAS tours expand one's understanding of New York's storied past and urban form rather than advocating for a new development or against a slated demolition.

MAS offers walking tours year-round, rain or shine. We are just as apt to tour Central Park or walk along the lower Manhattan shoreline in winter as we are to stroll through Forest Hills or Greenpoint in summer. We can be found looking at skyscrapers in midtown, or walking in Coney Island or Flushing, at any time of year. Go to www.mas.org to learn where to meet the week's walk exploring the physical form of the city and the forces that have shaped it.

Our first walking tour took place during a spring snowstorm; our fiftieth anniversary walk continued despite a steady downpour (fortunately, both the 1956 and 2006 walks ended at an historic tavern). We even had a tour during a nor'easter. A hardy tourist from Chicago and an equally hardy tour leader from Brooklyn pressed on through rain and wind, sheltering in doorways and behind leeward walls.

Although our first tours were limited to Manhattan, we now go to all five boroughs, from the northern end of the Bronx to the southernmost tip of Staten Island. Tours take participants to places they have never visited and to neighborhoods they once knew well. Tours are an opportunity to check out a neighborhood before you move there or to learn much more about the place where you already live.

It is the guide who makes or breaks a tour, whose combination of knowledge and personality can make a tour memorable. MAS has chosen to hire professionals rather than to train docents or students to follow a script. Coauthors Francis Morrone and Matthew A. Postal are the mainstays of the MAS tour program, each with his own fans. Francis is a classicist, while Matthew focuses on the modern era, and like good teachers everywhere, they are continually learning more about their subject, the amazing city that is New York.

Our other notable guides include Andrew Scott Dolkart, a member of the MAS Preservation Committee and director of Columbia University's Historic Preservation Program, well known for his own walking tour publications; Jack Eichenbaum, an urban geographer and world traveler; Justin Ferate, knowledgeable and charming about every borough; John Kriskiewicz, an expert on modernism and more; Sylvia Laudien-Meo, known for her art-related walking tours for adults and young people; Anthony W. Robins, an Art Deco authority and coauthor of *Subway Style*; and Joseph Svehlak, a passionate preservationist and native New Yorker. On occasion we use individuals who are not professionals, but they have detailed knowledge about their own communities and can offer an insider's perspective.

In addition to public tours, MAS has an extensive private tour program that is used by organizations from across the United States and abroad. We arrange walking and bus tours for all manner of students and retirees, alumni associations and private clubs, and even on occasion for a couple who would rather blow their budget on a guided walking tour than tickets to the theater. We have arranged tours for architects from Norway, Denmark, Germany, and Ireland; for cultural heritage travelers from Canada and Australia; for construction executives from Hong Kong; and for civic leaders from Prague.

Although MAS may have been the first organization in the city to offer walking tours on a regular basis, we were far from the last. Other groups have tied their tours to advocacy. (Friends of Cast-Iron Architecture were especially clever in the 1970s. Margot Gayle, the group's founder, distributed small magnets so that tour-takers could test the metal content of any facade they walked past.) Today, dozens of organizations and individuals offer tours for every taste, from neo-Gothic churches to chocolate sampling in pricey shops.

Creating this guidebook has been a collaborative effort involving MAS staff, funders, guides, and members. Kent L. Barwick, president emeritus, and Jean Tatge, chief operating officer, championed the book's development from its earliest stages; Lisa W. Alpert, Eve Baron, Phyllis Samitz Cohen, Jim Liao, Patricia McHugh, Kathy O'Callaghan, Dale Ramsey, Jonathan Sills, Jo Steffens, and former staff members Seth Johnson and Greg Studwell offered critical advice along the way. Many thanks to Juan Camilo Osorio, MAS senior GIS analyst/planner; his maps will enable users of this guide to find the sites described here. Genevieve R. Sherman, issues coordinator, traversed each route, standardized the walking directions, and made sure that the text, the directions, and the maps were in synch. Each staffer did his or her essential work with good humor and in a timely fashion. Particular thanks to Larry Blumberg for consistently serving as a sounding board.

Our gratitude to MAS member Edward A. Toran, who contributed his time and his talent in photography; his pictures illuminate these pages wonderfully and enhance the tours. Edward is a polymath with a background in design who shaped the book in its initial stages and whose computer skills made selecting and categorizing the images easier. He was there every step of the way.

Thank you to our editor Nancy Green at W. W. Norton & Company, who was enthusiastic about *10 Architectural Walks in Manhattan* from the beginning, and to Vani Kannan and Nancy Palmquist for their work. Abigail Sturges designed this attractive volume, which allows the reader to follow our walks.

This book was made possible by a grant from Furthermore: a program of the J. M. Kaplan Fund. We thank Joan K. Davidson particularly for her longtime support of MAS; it has been elemental, for in 1980 she was instrumental in the launching of Urban Center Books, MAS's popular architectural bookstore.

Finally, our profound thanks to Francis Morrone and Matthew A. Postal, who take such great pleasure in walking, looking, and explaining New York to anyone within proximity of their voices, oral and written. Their passion for exploring the city's buildings and neighborhoods and sharing that knowledge, just as Henry Hope Reed did more than fifty years ago on the first MAS tour, is the rationale for this MAS guidebook.

There can be only one response to all our efforts over the years: Go forth!

To contact MAS:
457 Madison Ave, New York, N.Y. 10022
ph (212) 935-3960
www.mas.org

# Reflections of a Tour Taker
## Stop and Smell the Gargoyles

ALLISON SILVER

Cities are about juxtaposition, and the greatest of cities are about sharp juxtapositions. Unlike people bump against each other on crowded streets; exotic spices from differing cultures blend together into the same dish. Most of all, contrasting buildings play off each other to create a syncopated urban rhythm.

And you experience this best by walking.

MAS figured this out a half-century ago, when it offered its first walking tour in 1956, and so set the template for the myriad tours offered today.

Walking down certain streets in New York can be intoxicating. A voluptuous Beaux-Arts wedding cake becomes more seductive when nestled beside an austere, glass-sheathed tower. The grace of an Italian Renaissance brickwork arch suddenly looks more artful opposite a trim Federal town house. The rococo of terra-cotta grows more giddy when it juts up against stolid cast-iron symmetry. A row of sedate brownstones can be charming, but it is more sweetly old-fashioned when you turn a corner and find a new steel and glass condo.

There is a joy that comes from walking in New York, from the unexpected pleasures that result when you have the time to stop and, most important, to look up. Look up and see the row of six bosomy caryatids supporting the top floors of a staid lower Fifth Avenue office building (1); see the light refracted by the rippling, nineteenth-century windowpanes on the floors above a modern storefront; see the row of elegant Ionic columns, a snowy capital, high atop the St. James Building (2), designed by Bruce Price. (He was a well-connected society architect and, as I learned on a walking tour, the father of Emily Post.)

The storied history of the city, in all its many layers, is right here, if you only take the time to look—and have the right guide. The sense of discovery is a delight, especially when you unlock secrets about buildings you think you know. During one walking tour, I learned that the weighty cast-iron buildings of Mercer

This voluptuous stone figure, which appears to support the structure above it, is one of six identical semi-covered caryatids positioned along the facade of a lower Fifth Avenue building.

Street were probably the sites of brothels in Walt Whitman's day. I now always stop at 155, a spare, former firehouse, where Francis Morrone, who led that tour, said Whitman had first met Ralph Waldo Emerson when the celebrated transcendental writer came down to New York to meet the author of *Leaves of Grass*.

When you take the time to stop, you see a building in a new way. One tour focused on Paul Rudolph, the hard-edged modernist responsible for just a few, choice buildings in New York—including Halston's famed town house at 101 East 63rd Street. Rudolph is one of those architects, like John Lautner, whose work would provide the perfect surroundings for a Bond villain. It has a deliciously dangerous feel. Literally so, since hanging staircases lack railings and balconies cantilever out into space. Rudolph specialized in the sort of house where taking a wrong step while, say, getting a glass of milk in the middle of the night can spell doom.

In what seemed like a colossal joke, Matthew A. Postal, who led this Rudolph tour, included Trump Tower (**3**). After all, it seemed clear that nothing could be further from Rudolph's stripped-down power than the gaudy frivolity of this structure's atrium. Until, that is, you really looked at it. There were the views into the

This modernist structure, formerly a nineteenth-century town house, was remodeled as the home and office of Swiss-born architect William Lescaze using white stucco, glass brick, and horizontal windows.

central space from varying levels, the strong water element, the cascading plants, the sharp balconies, the honed surfaces in sumptuous materials. Suddenly, you saw Rudolph everywhere. And, it turns out, Trump's architect, Der Scutt, was a protégé of Rudolph.

Of course, it helps if you like everything—or at least keep an open mind. Unless a city changes and grows, it's in amber or a theme park. Some New Yorkers are furious that Renzo Piano, one of most celebrated (and successful) contemporary architects, designed the addition to the Morgan Library (**4**); others fulminate about Edward Durell Stone ever being allowed to build that nutty Huntington Hartford museum on Columbus Circle (**5**); others rue the day that William Lescaze's 1934 International Style town house insinuated itself amid the placid brownstones of Turtle Bay (**6**). Some still mourn the loss of the original Waldorf=Astoria Hotel, a glorious pile replaced by that upstart Empire State Building (**7**).

So many New Yorkers remain scarred by the loss of buildings past. In their eyes, the graceful 1928 Italian Renaissance design by Cass Gilbert (of Woolworth Building fame) for the New York Life Insurance Company (**8**) can never measure up to Stanford White's flamboyant Madison Square Garden, torn down to make room for it. The destruction of McKim, Mead & White's Pennsylvania Station remains a seismic event in the city's psyche.

When it comes to buildings, I'm promiscuous. I love them all. All sizes, all styles, all eras. And walking tours let me see them all. I love James Renwick Jr.'s Calvary Church (**9**) and Wallace K. Harrison's Metropolitan Opera House (**10**); I love the two McKim, Mead & White buildings catty-corner to each other at Broadway and 20th Street, and Gordon Bunshaft's Lever House (**11**). (And I love Lever House even more knowing, as I learned from a MAS tour guide, that it was fostered by a senior executive at Lever Brothers who had worked at Johnson Wax and had experienced firsthand what an important building could do for a company. Not only had Frank Lloyd Wright's corporate headquarters in Racine, Wisconsin, bolstered the Johnson Wax brand far and wide, it had instilled pride and loyalty among the employees.)

I love the intricate marine motifs in the lobby of the Cunard Building (**12**), a remnant of the city's maritime glory, as much as the unadorned monolith that is Eero Saarinen's Black Rock (**13**). And I love that just two blocks from the sleek CBS tower, which somehow embodies America's sense of omnipotence in the early 1960s, is the Art Deco fantasy, Radio City Music Hall (**14**). I admit it, I even love the former Pan Am Building (**15**)—once a tour guide told me that Walter Gropius, the former head of the Bauhaus, had tried to fix it by shifting the building's orientation.

Such sharp juxtapositions are the essence of urban life. A certain cosmopolitan sophistication becomes ingrained when you are continually confronted by the unfamiliar and the offbeat. That's one reason people come to a city. Gradually, you learn to be unflappable, or else you couldn't make it through the day. You develop a special jadedness as a protective layer.

Yet, when you see a great building, the sheer joy it brings is heart-stopping. Walk down the stairway from Vanderbilt Avenue into Grand Central Terminal (**16**), under a starry canopy that is not quite blue and not quite green, and you have to pause at the grandeur of the main concourse. It's breathtaking. Stand at the edge of the plaza of the Seagram Building (**17**), bathed in a serenity created by Mies van der Rohe's bronze curtain wall, and you escape the daily hustle. Pass through the flurry of activity on the steps of Carrère & Hastings's New York Public Library (**18**) to enter the spectacular quiet of its Rose Main Reading Room.

But the pleasures can be smaller, and slyer. Once, as I was walking down a street with a high-powered Hollywood agent and his young son, the agent stopped to point out the row of small, oval, clerestory windows punctuating the top floor of a somewhat pedestrian town house. "See," he explained to the boy, "every building has something to offer."

Many cities in America are about driving—Los Angeles, for one. Its low-slung, Pop-art colored buildings register best through the window of a car. Main entrances regularly front the parking lot, not the street. But New York, the world's financial capital and media center, the furiously paced city that invented the streamlined modern era, is a throwback. The layers of its history are unveiled for the walker.

Your romance with the city only deepens as you unlock its secrets—when you know, for example, the locations of various buildings (what seems a shockingly large number) where Stanford White stashed a bevy of mistresses, or that there are so many London plane trees on the streets because it was Robert Moses's favorite, or that a patch of sidewalk in the East 70s was designed by the artist Alexander Calder (**19**). You love the city more as your awareness of it grows.

So to really understand New York, you have to walk it. And make sure to stop and look.

## Where to Stop and Smell the Gargoyles

1   Caryatids support the top-floor columns at **91 Fifth Avenue** *(Between 16th and 17th Streets)*. See page 15.

2   **St. James Building**, Bruce Price, 1896–98.
    *1133 Broadway (southwest corner of 26th Street)*

3   **Trump Tower**, Der Scutt of Swanke, Hayden & Connell, 1983.
    *725 Fifth Avenue (northeast corner of 56th Street)*

4   **Morgan Library and Museum**, Charles McKim of McKim, Mead & White; Benjamin Wistar Morris; Renzo Piano, 1903–6, 1928, 2006.
    *225 Madison Avenue (at 36th Street)*

5   Huntington Hartford's museum, the **Gallery of Modern Art**, by Edward Durell Stone (1964), redesigned by Brad Cloepfil of Allied Works Architecture for the Museum of Arts & Design, which held its groundbreaking in 2005.
    *2 Columbus Circle*

6.  **William Lescaze House and Office**, William Lescaze, 1933–34.
    *211 East 48th Street (between Second and Third Avenues)*. See page 16.

7   **Empire State Building**, Shreve, Lamb & Harmon, 1929–31.
    *350 Fifth Avenue (between 33rd and 34th Streets)*

8   **New York Life Insurance Company**, Cass Gilbert, 1926–28.
    *51 Madison Avenue (between 26th and 27th Streets).* See page 111.

9   **Calvary Church** (James Renwick Jr.), 1846.
    *277 Park Avenue South (northeast corner of 21st Street)*

10  **Metropolitan Opera House**, Wallace K. Harrison of Harrison & Abramovitz, 1966.
    Groundbreaking at Lincoln Center took place in late 1959. The Metropolitan Opera House
    was under construction during 1963. The official opening was on September 16, 1966, with
    the world premiere of Samuel Barber's *Antony and Cleopatra*.
    *Upper West Side, between West 62nd and 65th Streets and Columbus and Amsterdam Avenues*

11  **Lever House**, Gordon Bunshaft of Skidmore, Owings & Merrill, 1950–52.
    *390 Park Avenue (between 53rd and 54th Streets).* See pages 200, 202, 203.

12  **Cunard Building**, Benjamin Wistar Morris and Carrère & Hastings, 1917–21.
    *25 Broadway (on Bowling Green)*

13  **CBS Building**, Eero Saarinen & Associates, 1961–64; completed by Kevin Roche John
    Dinkeloo and Associates, 1965.
    *51 West 52nd Street (northeast corner of Sixth Avenue)*

14  **Radio City Music Hall**, The Associated Architects: Corbett, Harrison & MacMurray;
    Raymond Hood, Godley & Fouilhoux; Reinhard & Hofmeister; Donald Deskey, interiors;
    begun 1932.
    *1260 Sixth Avenue (between 50th and 51st Streets).* See pages 152, 153.

15  Former **Pan Am Building**, Emery Roth & Sons, Pietro Belluschi, and Walter Gropius,
    1958–63.
    *200 Park Avenue, just north of Grand Central Terminal.* See page 190.

16  **Grand Central Terminal**, Reed & Stem and Warren & Wetmore, 1903–13.
    *East 42nd Street at Park Avenue, north side.* See pages 158, 160, 161, 163.

17  **Seagram Building**, Mies van der Rohe, with Philip Johnson, 1955–58.
    *375 Park Avenue (between 52nd and 53rd Streets).* See pages 186, 187, 204, 205.

18  **New York Public Library**, Main Research Library, Carrère & Hastings, 1898–1911.
    *Fifth Avenue at 42nd Street*

19  **Alexander Calder sidewalk**, Alexander Calder, 1970.
    *1014–1018 Madison Avenue (between 78th and 79th Streets)*

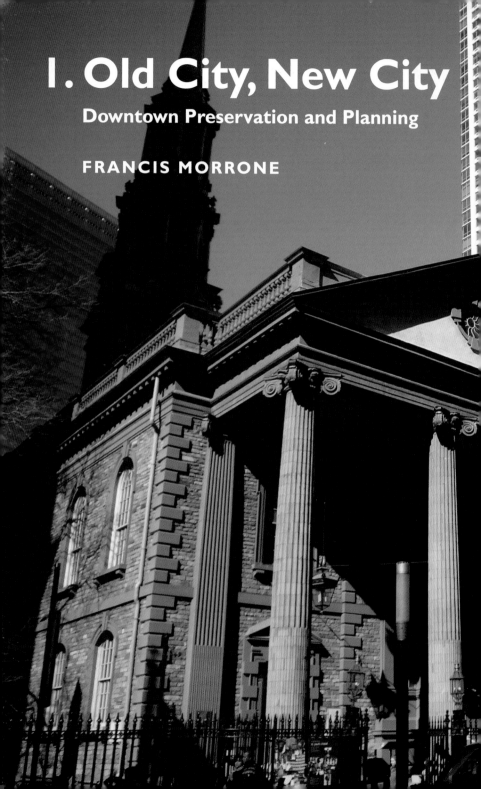

# 1. Old City, New City

## Downtown Preservation and Planning

### FRANCIS MORRONE

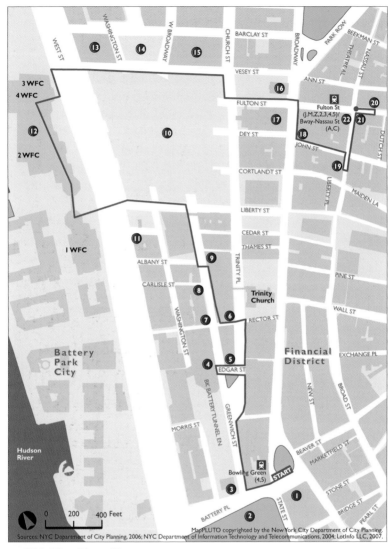

## Old City, New City: Downtown Preservation and Planning

1 former United States Custom House at 1 Bowling Green
2 Battery Park
3 Brooklyn-Battery Tunnel Ventilation Building
4 Battery Parking Garage
5 67 Greenwich Street
6 former U.S. Express headquarters
7 94, 94½, and 96 Greenwich Street
8 110 Greenwich Street
9 former Western Electric Co. factory
10 Ground Zero
11 90 West Street
12 Winter Garden
13 Barclay-Vesey Building
14 7 World Trade Center
15 Federal Office Building
16 St. Paul's Chapel
17 former American Telephone & Telegraph headquarters
18 Corbin Building
19 63 Nassau Street
20 Keuffel & Esser Building
21 Armeny Building
22 Fulton Building

**By Subway:** 4, 5 to Bowling Green
**By Bus:** M1, M6

egin in front of the former **United States Custom House** (1899–1907, Cass Gilbert) at the foot of Broadway. (1) The view north, across Bowling Green, is one of the most stirring and most exquisitely framed city views in the world. The art historian E. H. Gombrich wrote of elaborate picture frames that they are "a form of praise." The buildings that frame the northward view on Broadway are a form of praise for New York.

This walk, however, does not focus on icons or iconic views of New York, but on the process of change. Downtown, where New York began, hasn't stopped changing since the 1620s. Even the classic view from Bowling Green is only eighty or so years old, and in that time two buildings that were essential components of the classic picture—George B. Post's Produce Exchange and Ernest Flagg's Singer Tower—were demolished, the city's greatest losses of the last half-century, along with Pennsylvania Station.

But in the wake of the destruction of the World Trade Center on September 11, 2001, downtown has been in a state of intense churn, and this walk's purpose is to explore some lesser- and better-known byways that may yield lessons on how we manage—or should manage—change.

**Walk one block west along Battery Place to Greenwich Street.**

On your left is the 23-acre **Battery Park.** (2) The park was created by the progressive extension of the shoreline by landfill from the late eighteenth century to the 1870s. The name refers to a gun battery established in the late seventeenth century by the Dutch West India Company along the shore, which was then just outside Fort Amsterdam, on the site of the former Custom House. The dominant structure in the park, the circular stone fort called Castle Clinton, was completed in 1811 as part of a series of harbor defenses. It was originally called West Battery and was 200 feet offshore. It was still offshore when, on September 11, 1850, P.T. Barnum presented the "Swedish Nightingale," soprano Jenny Lind, in concert at what was then called Castle Garden. Later, from 1855 to 1890, the fort served as the immigrant processing depot, until a new facility was established on Ellis Island in the harbor. McKim, Mead & White remodeled Castle Clinton into the New York Aquarium, which flourished on the site from 1896 to 1941. For many years it was the most visited attraction in New York City. Castle Clinton was nearly torn down by master builder Robert Moses when he planned to construct a Brooklyn-Battery Bridge that would have obliterated Battery Park. Instead, he built the Brooklyn-Battery Tunnel, construction of which caused much of Battery Park to be closed throughout the 1940s. In the process of building the tunnel, Moses completely redesigned the park. He relocated the New York Aquarium to Coney Island, and he gave the park its present, distinctive formal design. (Moses favored formal gardens over the naturalistic greenswards that Calvert Vaux and Frederick Law Olmsted had made the traditional style of New York City parks.)

Tunnel-related structures also came to dominate the park periphery along Battery Place. At the northwest corner of Battery Place and Greenwich Street stands one of the tunnel's **ventilation buildings**. (3) It was built in 1950 in the chaste, vaguely classical style that Moses favored and that his architect, Aymar Embury II, perfected. Embury, incidentally, had once worked for Cass Gilbert, architect of the nearby Custom House. (The ventilation building has become an unlikely tourist destination after being featured in the 1997 movie *Men in Black*.)

**Turn right onto Greenwich Street to Morris Street to view the Battery Parking Garage.**

The tunnel made such a hash of this southernmost part of Greenwich Street that it's hard to believe this was once the most fashionable residential thoroughfare in the city. To the north of the ventilation building is the large **Battery Parking Garage** from 1950, a striking modernist design by the tunnel's engineer, Ole Singstad. (4) What Othmar Ammann was to New York's bridges (he designed most of them), the Norwegian-born Ole Singstad was to the city's tunnels, with credits including the Holland, Lincoln, and Queens-Midtown tunnels as well as the Brooklyn-Battery. Yet, however much we may admire Singstad's handiwork, the great fuming gash of access ramps cries out for civic improvement, which at this writing has been promised as part of the city's master plan for downtown.

This late eighteenth-century mansion at the foot of Greenwich Street belonged to Robert Dickey, one of the city's richest men; it exemplifies the Federal style.

**Continue north bearing to the right. Turn west on Edgar Street and cross back to Greenwich Street to view 67 Greenwich Street on the northeast corner of the intersection.**

In his 1880 novel *Washington Square*, set in the 1840s, Henry James wrote of his protagonist Dr. Sloper's late wife:

> Mrs. Sloper was amiable, graceful, accomplished, elegant, and in 1820 she had been one of the pretty girls of the small but promising capital which clustered about the Battery and overlooked the Bay, and of which the uppermost boundary was indicated by the grassy waysides of Canal Street.

Our principal reminder of the halcyon residential days of Greenwich Street is just across the street from the garage. The house at **67 Greenwich Street**, at the northeast corner of the short, block-long Edgar Street (named for no one is quite sure whom), dates from 1809–10, a rare Manhattan survivor from the early years of the republic. (**5**) (According to the Landmarks Preservation Commission, only seven houses from 1810 or earlier still stand south of Chambers Street, and four of them are on Greenwich Street.) The line of Greenwich Street was the original Hudson shoreline, and the street had only been opened in 1797, according to research by Jay Shockley of the Landmarks Preservation Commission.

Greenwich Street soon became known as "Millionaire's Row," home to members of many of the socially most prominent families in the city. For example, Mayor De Witt Clinton lived at 82 Greenwich Street (in a house no longer standing).

The house at 67 Greenwich was built by a merchant named Robert Dickey and his wife, Anne. At 40 feet wide it qualifies as a mansion in Manhattan. Indeed, Dickey was one of the richest men in the city. As was not unusual at the time, he conducted his business from the same building in which he resided. The residence fronted on Greenwich; the business on Lumber Street (present-day Trinity Place). The house's history tracks that of the residential Battery as a whole. The Dickeys lived there until 1820. It soon after became a boarding house, at first for well-to-do boarders, then for working-class boarders as fashionable society abandoned the neighborhood for such areas as present-day SoHo and Greenwich Village. In 1871 the police raided 67 Greenwich as a "house of ill fame." A year later the originally 3½-story house was raised to a full fourth story, and some other alterations were made, including a new entrance on Greenwich Street, designed by the major nineteenth-century architect Detlef Lienau.

As the house was converted to commercial uses, owners gave no priority to aesthetic maintenance, and decay and encrustations eventually obscured the house's historical importance, especially as most of its Greenwich Street brethren were lost, some of them to the tunnel construction. The Landmarks Preservation Commission held a hearing on the house in 1965, the commission's first year in existence, but failed to designate it. Designation finally came forty years later, amid fear that the house might be lost to downtown redevelopment. Look closely, though, and you will see the features of the Federal style, such as the Flemish-bond brickwork (now painted over) and the beautiful splayed lintels, with raised keystones, over the windows. Walk round to the Trinity Place side to see the rare bowed front. The Federal style made wide use of curving or elliptical forms, and oval rooms were fashionable in the late eighteenth and early nineteenth centuries, though less so, it seems, in New York than in other places. That makes the bowed front on Trinity Place all the more precious. You must, of course, look past the single-story commercial structure that fills in what used to be the house's yard.

### Return east on Edgar Street to Trinity Place.

Trinity Place has a unique character as the back alley of Broadway. The buildings on the east side of the street are the backs of buildings on Broadway—between Exchange Alley (which connects Edgar Street to Exchange Place on the other side of Broadway) and Rector Street we see the rears of the former Adams Express

Building (61 Broadway) by Francis H. Kimball (architect of the Corbin Building, which we will see later on this walk) from 1912–13, the former American Express Building (65 Broadway) by Renwick, Aspinwall & Tucker from 1914–19, and the Empire Building (71 Broadway) by Francis H. Kimball from 1896–98. As they front Broadway, these are all very grand buildings. Behind them on Trinity Place are their utilitarian annexes. Next door to the rear of 67 Greenwich is the building, now the discount clothier Syms, that once housed the Adams Express Co.'s stables. It was built around 1870. Located two buildings to the north, opposite the rear of the American Express Building, is the 1885 American Express Co. warehouse, a distinctive Romanesque Revival structure with superb brickwork, designed by the major architect Edward H. Kendall. Adams Express and American Express were, with Wells Fargo, the three principal financial-industry express-delivery firms of the nineteenth century; all three still exist, having grown into diversified financial services companies.

**Walk north on Trinity Place to Rector Street to view 2 Rector Street at the northwest corner of the intersection.**

Extending to Greenwich Street, this remarkable and almost hidden skyscraper, designed by the outstanding Clinton & Russell, was built in 1905–7 with gleaming terra-cotta facades predating those of the Woolworth Building by several years. Originally the headquarters of **U.S. Express** (which competed with Adams Express and American Express), the 26-story building later was home to EBASCO, the gas and electric holding company that so dominated the energy industry that in the 1930s its restructuring was mandated by the federal government. (**6**)

These late-eighteenth-century townhouses on Greenwich Street are, above their commercial ground floors, in remarkably intact condition.

**Return west to Greenwich Street.**

At the northwest corner of Rector Street stand a trio of four-story houses—
**94, 94½,** and **96 Greenwich Street**—that, according to the New York Landmarks Conservancy, date from 1798. (**7**) They are not nearly as grand as 67
Greenwich, but they are older and, above their commercialized ground floors, are
more intact. It's one of the wonders of New York that street-level visual cacoph-
ony often yields to history only one floor above, left untouched solely because
nobody wished to pay to spoil it. At this writing, these houses have not been
designated by the Landmarks Preservation Commission.

**Walk one block north to Carlisle Street to view 110 Greenwich
Street at the southwest corner.**

A strikingly modern loft building dating from 1928–29, **110 Greenwich
Street** was designed by William Higginson, who may have been the most prolific
industrial architect in New York history. (**8**) Directly to its south at 108 Greenwich
is the site of the home of George Templeton Strong (1820–1875), lawyer, aesthete, and diarist, who has been called New York's Samuel Pepys. In 1845 he wrote

The loft building at
110 Greenwich Street was
designed by William Higginson
who, though his name is little
known to the public, was one
of the most prolific and
innovative designers of early
twentieth-century industrial
buildings in New York.

in his diary about how bad his Greenwich Street neighborhood was getting and how he was soon going to move. He did. In 1848 he moved from here to East 21st Street.

**Continue north to Thames Street to view the former Western Electric Co. factory at the southeast corner.**

Designed in 1888–89 by Cyrus L. W. Eidlitz, son of the great New York architect Leopold Eidlitz and architect of the Times Tower at Times Square, this was one of the city's earliest telephone factories. (**9**) Western Electric Company is also one of the handsomest Romanesque Revival industrial buildings in the city, kin to the American Express warehouse we saw earlier. It's fascinating to think that once upon a time factories operated in the shadow of the glamorous towers of the Financial District.

**Continue north two blocks to Liberty Street. At last we come to Ground Zero.**

Four blocks of Greenwich Street, from Liberty to Vesey Streets, were demapped when the World Trade Center superblock was created in the late 1960s and early 1970s. (**10**) At the northwest corner of Greenwich and Liberty

Western Electric manufactured telephone equipment in this building, erected in the 1880s. It reminds us that factories once flourished in the shadow of the financial center.

The view across Ground Zero from the east shows, from left to right, Cesar Pelli's World Financial Center towers; Ralph Walker's New York Telephone Company Building; and Skidmore, Owings & Merrill's replacement for 7 World Trade Center.

The former East River Savings Bank became Century 21, a famous discount department store that's a rare remnant of the old "Radio Row" days before the World Trade Center was built.

stood 2 World Trade Center, the tower with the observation deck. Remember that Greenwich was the original shoreline. That means that a bit more than half of the World Trade Center was constructed on landfill. To the west, on the other side of West Street, the vast mixed-use Battery Park City/World Financial Center complex was built, beginning in the 1980s, on new landfill, some of which came from excavations for the World Trade Center—meaning that some of Battery Park City stands on landfill made from excavated earlier landfill. Thus do cities grow.

The part of the World Trade Center site that has been with us always is bounded by Greenwich, Liberty, Church, and Vesey Streets. From farmland in Dutch times this became, throughout the English period, a densely populated, thriving neighborhood of artisans whose residences also included their workshops. (Duncan Phyfe lived and made his furniture in this neighborhood.) This was immediately south of King's (later Columbia) College, and is where the undergraduate Alexander Hamilton made a name for himself by his revolutionary exhortations in neighborhood taverns. The Great Fire of September 21, 1776, devastated the city to the west of Broadway, destroying perhaps all the buildings on what at the time existed of the future site of the World Trade Center. Following the Revolution, the city rebounded with stunning rapidity. By the middle of the nineteenth century the area was primarily industrial—such buildings as the Western Electric Co. factory we saw earlier remind us of this. The northern part of the World Trade Center site came to be occupied by Washington Market, which eventually extended all the way north to North Moore Street in what we now call TriBeCa. At one time the largest wholesale food market in the country, Washington Market was relocated to the Bronx in 1967 and renamed Hunt's Point Market. In the twentieth century, much of the area emerged as a retailing district renowned for its many dealers in electronic equipment and components, and was known as "Radio Row." This was also an area of discount merchandisers, a reminder of which is the popular Century 21 discount department store that has operated since 1961 in the former East River Savings Bank by Walker & Gillette from 1935, at the northeast corner of Church and Cortlandt Streets. Many were the New Yorkers who mourned the loss of Radio Row when the World Trade Center was built.

**Turn west on Liberty Street and ascend the stairs to the South Bridge, which extends over West Street into the World Financial Center. Pause on the bridge to view 90 West Street, on the southeast corner of Cedar Street.**

**90 West Street,** also known as the West Street Building is one of downtown's most beautiful buildings. (11) It was designed by Cass Gilbert in 1905–7,

Cass Gilbert's lovely West Street Building sustained terrible damage from the September 11, 2001, attacks, but was restored and converted to residences.

the exact years of Clinton & Russell's U.S. Express headquarters that we saw earlier. Gilbert's use of reedy terra-cotta piers riding up to a green mansard roof borrows the trick used by Louis Sullivan in his Bayard Building (1897–99, Bleecker at Crosby Streets) to make his tall building a "proud and soaring thing." Gilbert's facades also have a rich, filigreed character that is unusual for skyscraper curtain walls. Damaged on 9/11, the building faced an uncertain future but has been successfully converted from office to residential use and looks as good as ever. Its survival has been credited to excellent construction and the fire-retardant qualities of its extensive terra-cotta.

**Proceed across the bridge into the World Financial Center.**

Directly across West Street stands 1 World Financial Center, part of the complex of four office towers plus the Winter Garden atrium built in 1985–88. Architect Cesar Pelli designed the top of 1 World Financial Center as a stylized mansard roof in tribute to 90 West Street. To the north, 2 and 3 World Financial Center (with, respectively, the domed and the pyramidal tops) stand directly across from Ground Zero. Between them is the Winter Garden.

**Cross the skybridge over Liberty Street and continue straight through the corridors of 2 World Financial Center. Descend into the Winter Garden.**

The greenhouse-like **Winter Garden** encloses a space as big as Grand Central Terminal's main concourse. (**12**) With its sixteen palm trees, benches, and sunniness, the Winter Garden is by day a reposeful respite for office workers, while on nights and weekends it becomes a place of cultural programming and performances. Before September 11, 2001, the grand stairway at the east end led to an aerial bridge over West Street to 6 World Trade Center. Not only was the bridge destroyed on that terrible day, so too was the Winter Garden itself. That it was rebuilt and reopened within a year was indescribably heartening to New Yorkers. Today the east end has been redesigned as a viewing platform from which one can look directly down on to Ground Zero.

At this writing there is little to see on the 16-acre Ground Zero site, beyond the grim fascination of the exposed steel support beams of the "slurry wall," built to keep river water from filling the excavated "bathtub," as the engineers called it, of the site. Before long, we hope, a new complex will rise. Current plans involve four rather glitzy skyscrapers, each by a major international architect. The "Freedom Tower" will be the tallest. Originally designed by the Bronx High School of

Science–educated Daniel Libeskind, its design has been significantly altered by David Childs of Skidmore, Owings & Merrill. The other towers are being designed by Britain's Norman Foster and Richard Rogers and Japan's Fumihiko Maki. An elaborate memorial by Michael Arad and Peter Walker, a cultural center by the Norwegian architects Snøhetta, and—most eagerly anticipated by most people— a new PATH station by the brilliant Spanish engineer/architect Santiago Calatrava will round out the complex.

To the west outside the Winter Garden is World Financial Center Plaza, looking out on the Hudson River. Designed by landscape architect M. Paul Friedberg with artists Scott Burton and Siah Armajani, the plaza overflows with café tables and a variety of seating that make it one of Manhattan's most pleasant spots for a weekday lunch in fine weather. Battery Park City, with its several parks and artworks, and especially with its beguiling riverfront esplanade, is well worth exploring, though it is too much to describe in the context of this walk.

**Circle around to the back of the staircase and exit onto West Street. Look to the northern edge of Ground Zero to view the former New York Telephone Co. Building at the northeast corner of West and Vesey Streets. Immediately to its east is 7 World Trade Center.**

The New York Telephone Co. Building (now Verizon), also known as the

The New York Telephone Co. Building, one of the first Art Deco skyscrapers and one of architect Ralph Walker's several masterpieces in New York, was badly damaged on September 11, 2001, but has been saved and restored.

**Barclay-Vesey Building**, from 1923–27 was designed by Ralph Walker of McKenzie, Voorhees & Gmelin. (**13**) Walker was one of the most imaginative skyscraper architects who ever lived. Besides this building, his masterpieces include One Wall Street, at Broadway, and Brooklyn's New York Telephone Co. Building, on Willoughby Street. With the Barclay-Vesey Building he helped pioneer the dramatic sculptural arrangement of the stepped-back masses that were mandated by the zoning law of 1916. He was also among the first to apply extensively the new ornamentation imported from France that would, in the 1960s, be dubbed "Art Deco." This outstanding building—notable as well for its beautiful tile-vaulted sidewalk arcades—once dominated the lower Manhattan skyline view from the Hudson River. But when the World Trade Center stood, the Barclay-Vesey Building seemed like a small puppy at the feet of the Twin Towers. This was another building that was badly damaged on 9/11 and that, for a while, seemed beyond rehabilitation. But careful restoration has brought it back to life.

Right on the line of Greenwich Street stands the new **7 World Trade Center**. (**14**) The old one, which was destroyed on 9/11, was not part of the original six-building complex but rather was added in the 1980s. The new one, designed by David Childs of Skidmore, Owings & Merrill for the developer Larry Silverstein, is a sleek modern building that at first no one seemed eager to move into but that has, in fact, established itself as a premier office address. It's well to point out that, though New Yorkers worried deeply about downtown in the wake of 9/11, and though, at this writing, Ground Zero remains a hole in the ground, in general this neighborhood not only has bounced back but has positively boomed, in terms of both offices and residences.

**Turn north on West Street to Vesey Street. Cross the bridge over West Street and continue east past 7 World Trade Center to West Broadway to view the Federal Office Building.**

Spanning Vesey Street from West Broadway to Church Street, the handsome **Federal Office Building** was designed by Cross & Cross and Pennington & Lewis and built in 1933–35. (**15**)

**Continue east to Church Street and turn south to Fulton Street.**

Ground Zero is on your right. Note the temporary PATH station, which will be replaced by a permanent one designed by Santiago Calatrava. PATH stands for Port Authority Trans-Hudson, a railroad that serves commuters from New Jersey. It was originally called the Hudson & Manhattan Railroad and was the first railroad

While redevelopment proved painfully slow on the main World Trade Center site, developer Larry Silverstein and architect David Childs built the gleaming new 7 World Trade Center across Vesey Street.

successfully to tunnel under the Hudson River between New Jersey and New York. The Hudson & Manhattan established a depot here underneath the twin 22-story Hudson Terminal Buildings (1907–9, Clinton & Russell), which stood on the west side of Church Street between Fulton and Cortlandt Streets (with Dey Street running between them). The "original twin towers," which were demolished for the World Trade Center, were a prominent presence in a largely low-rise part of town. In 1962, when the Hudson & Manhattan faced bankruptcy, the Port Authority of New York and New Jersey, which had been created in 1921 as a super-governmental agency to coordinate port activities between the two states on either side of the Hudson River, purchased the railroad, fearing that its failure would be catastrophic for the metropolitan transit system. That's the short story of how the Port Authority acquired this land—which came with the railroad—and wound up as the developer of the World Trade Center. The complex was officially dedicated in 1973. Twenty years later, terrorists came very close to destroying the complex. Eight years after that, terrorists who commandeered two jetliners succeeded in doing what the 1993 bombers had failed to do.

**Across Church Street from Ground Zero, between Vesey and Fulton Streets, is lovely St. Paul's Chapel, one of all-too-few colonial survivors in Manhattan.**

**St. Paul's Chapel** was built to serve Trinity Parish's "uptown" congregants. (16) When the chapel opened for services in 1766 it faced west, toward the Hudson River. Two years later, the stately Broadway portico was added, with its four fluted Ionic columns made of brown sandstone supporting a broad triangular pediment in the center of which a niche, with a rounded pediment, holds a statue of St. Paul. The chapel's exterior walls are of local schist. Inside, the pastel color scheme, the original Waterford chandeliers, and the large Palladian window all testify to the nonsacramental Anglicanism the later Gothic Revival rebelled against. This could as easily be the setting of a cotillion as of a worship service. In 1789, after George Washington took the oath of office as America's first president, he and his party attended a service at St. Paul's; needless to say, the Te Deum, in those days, was recited not sung—the architecture would suggest as much. (At the 1865 memorial service for President Lincoln at the Gothic Trinity Church on Broadway at Wall Street, the Te Deum was sung.) George and Martha Washington worshipped here on Sundays when the capital remained in New York; their box pew in the north aisle bears the requisite plaque. Above the pew, the oil painting is the oldest known representation of the Great Seal of the United States. Striking a

St. Paul's Chapel, one of New York's few extant colonial buildings, survived the Great Fire of 1776, was President and Mrs. Washington's church, and survived the attacks on the World Trade Center, right across Church Street.

different note, the cornet and feathers surmounting the pulpit are the only symbols of British royalty remaining in their original location in New York. The Hebrew lettering on the wall was not unusual in the Anglican Church at the time. By the time of St. Paul's, James Gibbs, architect of London's St Martin-in-the-Fields, had replaced Christopher Wren as the principal form giver to British architecture. Gibbs designed buildings and produced pattern books that suggested to local vernacular builders how they might build—or provided them with detailed plans for buildings. Thus we say that St. Paul's is a Georgian church in the Gibbs mode. In 1793 a high tower was added to St. Paul's. Its design, adapted from the Choragic Monument of Lysicrates, may be the oldest extant example of "Grecian" architecture in New York, drawn from James Stuart and Nicholas Revett's monumental *Antiquities of Athens*.

St. Paul's survived the Great Fire of September 21, 1776—one of very few buildings to the west of Broadway that did. Remarkably, it also survived the attacks of September 11, 2001. As the search for survivors and the cleanup of the site proceeded through the fall of 2001, St. Paul's served the round-the-clock workers as a place of rest and refreshment, where they could nap, get a massage, or listen to soothing music. Such was St. Paul's role in those weeks that the chapel has become the city's de facto 9/11 memorial as we await the official one at Ground Zero.

**Walk east along the north side of Fulton Street to the northeast corner of Broadway to view 195 Broadway on the southwest corner.**

The magnificent 195 Broadway was originally the headquarters of **American Telephone & Telegraph.** (17) AT&T's legendary leader Theodore Vail commissioned the design from William Welles Bosworth.

Unlike McKim, Mead & White or Cass Gilbert, Bosworth did not produce a catalog of Manhattan buildings familiar to us all. He often worked for the Rockefellers. He laid out the campus of Rockefeller Institute (now Rockefeller University) on the Upper East Side, and he was the principal designer of the house and grounds at Kykuit, in Pocantico Hills, New York. Under Rockefeller patronage, Bosworth took on the restoration of France's war-ravaged landmarks, including the palace at Versailles and the cathedral at Rheims. In Manhattan, Bosworth sensitively adapted Morton Plant's mansion into the Cartier store on Fifth Avenue at 52nd Street.

William Welles Bosworth, one of New York's greatest architects, designed the headquarters of American Telephone & Telegraph as a conjectural adaptation of the long-lost third-century Septizodium on Rome's Palatine hill.

Bosworth's masterpiece may be 195 Broadway. No more distinctive sky-scraper graces New York. Built in phases between 1913 and 1924, the building rises in a series of great granite colonnades. The form may be a conjectural adaptation of the long-lost Septizodium on the Palatine hill in Rome of the third century A.D. But the keynote is Greek. Here the Doric forms the base, as it should, the simplicity and strength of its capitals suiting it to the projection of muscularity. Above the order, as writer and architectural historian Henry Hope Reed points out, the elegant Ionic order is that of the temple of Artemis-Cybele in Sardis, from the fourth century B.C.

As impressive as is Bosworth's exterior, his lobby is as fine as that in any office building in the country. Often described as a "forest" of columns, the marble lobby is indescribably majestic. (See pages 62, 63.) The columns are the Doric of the Parthenon, repeated and ranked in a glorious phantasm of temple architecture. The Doric severity finds relief in Bosworth's wealth of meticulous details, in great bronze chandeliers, in brass rails, and in sculpture by Paul Manship, Chester Beach, and Gaston Lachaise.

At this writing, the east side of Broadway across from 195 is a thundering mess of construction as the city builds its Fulton Street Transit Center, designed by the British firm of Sir Nicholas Grimshaw with the artist James Carpenter. Unfortunately, the most eagerly anticipated aspect of the design, Carpenter's great glass dome, has been abandoned because of rapidly escalating costs. The block on which the Transit Center is being built contained several distinctive old buildings, of which preservationists succeeded in having the Corbin Building—the most important one in the group—saved.

**Walk south on Broadway to the northeast corner of John Street.**

At the northeast corner of Broadway and John Street stands the **Corbin Building** of 1888–89. (**18**) It is 20 feet wide on Broadway and 161 feet deep on John Street. Francis H. Kimball, one of the most inventive New York architects of the late nineteenth century, designed it in a powerfully picturesque variant of the "arcaded" style of skyscraper design of that era. It is truly one of the most important and most beautiful of Manhattan's very early skyscrapers still standing. (See page 60.)

**Walk east on John Street to Nassau Street. Turn south and stop midblock to view 63 Nassau Street on the west side of the street.**

**63 Nassau Street** is a cast-iron-fronted building designed by James Bogardus (1800–1874) from c. 1857–59, as ascertained by Landmarks Preservation Commission research that led to the building's belated landmark designation in 2007. (**19**) Bogardus was an inventor and builder and a pioneer of cast-iron architecture. The Landmarks Preservation Commission says that, in the entire country, only five Bogardus buildings are known to be still standing. One of his most famous, the Laing Store, which stood from 1848 to 1971 at Washington and Murray Streets, was dismantled rather than demolished and was placed in storage with the intention that it would be re-erected as part of the South Street Seaport development in the 1980s. The iron facade elements, however, were stolen. In its place, Beyer Blinder Belle designed a new building there called the Bogardus Building. Nonetheless, we have what we believe is an authentic Bogardus right here, very near the seaport. The cast-iron facade was apparently added to a much older building.

**Return north to Fulton Street and walk east midblock to view number 127 on the north side of the street.**

The **Keuffel & Esser Building** of 1891 was designed by De Lemos & Cordès. (**20**) Ask any old engineer about Keuffel & Esser, and his eyes will light up. As a student, the engineer probably had to make do with a cheap slide rule. As he prospered, he switched to the best: a Keuffel & Esser. Two German immigrants founded the company, which in 1891 became the first in America to manufacture slide rules. Their plant was in Hoboken, New Jersey. But their offices were at 127 Fulton Street. Today, the building, obscured by grime and signage, barely registers to passersby on the motley thoroughfare that connects the South Street Seaport to Ground Zero. Look closely, though, and you'll see a gem of a building, one that if it were restored might shine as it did when Keuffel and Esser hired their countryman, Theodore De Lemos, to design it in 1891. The building boasts a magnificent cast-iron storefront, ornamented with delicate images of Keuffel & Esser products. Above this rises a section in brick and stone, defined by a bold arch. Above that rises a three-sided oriel. It's all lavishly embellished and, like the Corbin Building, a product of perhaps the most picturesque phase of American architecture.

De Lemos & Cordès were the city's greatest department store architects. Their works include the former Siegel Cooper Store, on Sixth Avenue between 18th and 19th Streets (where Bed, Bath & Beyond now is), the former Adams Dry-Goods Store, on Sixth Avenue between 21st and 22nd streets, and Macy's 1902 building facing Herald Square at 34th Street and Broadway.

De Lemos & Cordès's picturesque building incorporates imagery
of Keuffel & Esser's once-renowned scientific instruments.

The Armeny Building joins with the Fulton Building and the Keuffel & Esser Building to make this stretch of Fulton Street "De Lemos & Cordès country." The firm was also famous for department stores, such as Macy's at Herald Square.

## Return to the corner of Fulton and Nassau Streets.

This corner is the place to savor De Lemos & Cordès's work. In addition to the Keuffel & Esser Building, they designed the **Armeny Building**, at the southeast corner, in 1889, and the **Fulton Building**, at the southwest corner, in

1891–93. (**21, 22**) Each of these buildings is exciting. They kept their own offices in the Fulton Building, which, with its rounded corner, negotiates the intersection with true majesty.

In 1967, for their centennial, Keuffel & Esser sponsored a survey of scientists, asking for predictions of what the world would be like in 2067. We would live in domed cities, and such. The futurists failed to predict the imminent demise of Keuffel & Esser's best-known product. By the early 1970s, the company ceased production of slide rules, as electric calculators became standard. A California company absorbed Keuffel & Esser in the 1980s. The Keuffel & Esser Building was designated by the Landmarks Preservation Commission in 2005.

On Greenwich and Fulton Streets, and even on Broadway (in the case of the Corbin Building), the virtues of significant older buildings have often been obscured by changing uses, lack of care, or gaudy signage. Yet no comprehensive planning for a better downtown can fail to find a place for many of these wonderful works of architecture.

**Leaving**

**By Subway:** 2, 3, J, M, Z at Fulton Street; A, C at Broadway-Nassau Street
**By Bus:** M1, M6

## Suggested Reading

*American Buildings and Their Architects, Vol. 1: The Colonial and Neoclassical Styles*, by William H. Pierson. Oxford University Press, 1970. Though not specific to New York, this is the best book for understanding Colonial, Federal, and Greek Revival architecture in America.

*Diary*, by George Templeton Strong, edited by Allan Nevins and Milton Halsey Thomas. The Macmillan Company, 1952. Four volumes of the diaries of "New York's Samuel Pepys," covering the 1840s through the 1870s. Lawyer and aesthete, Strong lived on Greenwich Street in its heyday—and after.

*Divided We Stand: A Biography of New York's World Trade Center*, by Eric Darton. Basic Books, 1999. A thorough history of how the World Trade Center came to be, and the role it played in the life of the city once it was built.

*Inventing the Skyline: The Architecture of Cass Gilbert*, edited by Margaret Heilbrun. Columbia University Press, 2000. An excellently illustrated collection of essays by several scholars on aspects of the career of the architect of the United States Custom House, the West Street Building, and the Woolworth Building.

*Rise of the New York Skyscraper*, 1865–1913, by Sarah Bradford Landau and Carl W. Condit. Yale University Press, 1996. A magnificent book on the early skyscraper, including important examples along the route of this tour.

# 2. Before the Code

## Downtown Skyscrapers

### MATTHEW A. POSTAL

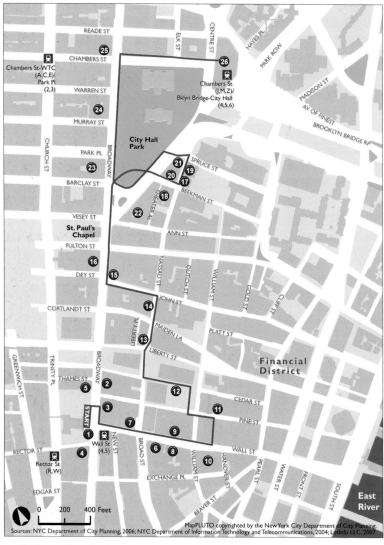

## Before the Code: Downtown Skyscrapers

1 Trinity Church
2 Equitable Building
3 former American Surety Company Building
4 Empire Building
5 Trinity Building
6 23 Wall Street
7 Bankers Trust Building
8 former Trust Company of America
9 former Bank of Manhattan Company
10 55 Wall Street
11 56 Pine Street
12 JPMorgan Chase Tower
13 Liberty Tower
14 63 Nassau Street
15 Corbin Building
16 former American Telephone & Telegraph headquarters
17 Morse Building
18 Temple Court Building
19 former American Tract Society
20 Potter Building
21 former New York Times Building
22 Park Row Building
23 Woolworth Building
24 Home Life Insurance Company Building
25 Broadway-Chambers Building
26 Municipal Building

**By Subway:** 4, 5 to Wall Street; R, W to Rector Street
**By Bus:** M1, M6

## Start in front of Trinity Church on the west side of Broadway where it meets Wall Street.

Prior to the Industrial Revolution, the tallest structures were church spires. Constructed without benefit of modern engineering techniques, these slender pinnacles pointed skyward, creating Manhattan's first skyline. For fifty years, **Trinity Church** stood the tallest, reaching an impressive height of about 280 feet. (1) Established in 1693, the present church is the third structure to occupy the site and was designed by Richard M. Upjohn in the Gothic Revival style between 1839 and 1846. The spire, near Broadway, contains a winding staircase. Before the introduction of elevators, nineteenth-century visitors would climb more than three hundred rickety steps, peering out small windows to attain unsurpassed views of the growing city.

## Walk north toward Pine Street, and stand opposite 120 Broadway.

Skyscrapers are more than just tall; they are usually defined as buildings that contain office space; have a fire-resistant skeleton, such as steel or concrete; and have passenger elevators. Though Chicago has long claimed the title as having the earliest skyscraper—the Home Insurance Company Building of 1885 (demolished)—in recent years New York City has received credit for the Equitable Life Assurance Company Building, which stood at 120 Broadway, between Pine and Cedar Streets, from 1870 to 1912. Though only 7½ stories tall, at 142 feet it was taller than neighboring commercial buildings, and the upper stories in the mansard roof offered views of the Hudson River and New Jersey. Most importantly, it was

Completed in 1846, Trinity Church was a pioneering example of the Gothic Revival style, influencing the character of religious buildings throughout the nation.

Set between Pine and Cedar Streets, the 42-story Equitable Building was New York's last unregulated skyscraper design.

the first office building planned with a passenger elevator, making all floors equally desirable. Expanded during the 1880s by architects Gilman & Kendall and George B. Post, it grew to include a through-block corridor to Nassau Street, memorably decorated with mosaics and stained glass. In this early lobby tenants and guests could wait for elevators, buy a newspaper, or send a telegram.

The subsequent **Equitable Building**, handsomely designed in the neo-Renaissance style by Ernest R. Graham & Associates, was completed in 1915. (2) It, too, was extremely important in the development of the skyscraper. Filling an entire block, this massive, 42-story building rises without setbacks, casting thick shadows along Pine Street for all but one or two hours each day. Built at a time when there was increasing concern about the effect that tall buildings were having on the urban environment, it led to the passage of the 1916 zoning code, requiring that subsequent towers decrease in mass as they rise. This law, which shaped the profiles of many of the city's most famous buildings, remained in effect until 1961.

South of Pine Street, at 100 Broadway, stands the former **American Surety Company Building**. (3) A classic and influential design, this Renaissance Revival

A row of robed maidens by sculptor J. Massey Rhind enlivens the base of the former American Surety Building.

structure was completed in 1896. Designed by Bruce Price, one of the most successful architects of his day, the granite elevations were treated as if they were classical columns. Whereas earlier skyscrapers often had a strong horizontal orientation, in which individual floors were neatly stacked in repetition without any sense of vertical integration, 100 Broadway employs a tripartite arrangement—base/shaft/capital—emphasizing the lower floors and a Ionic colonnade (with figures by sculptor J. Massey Rhind) as well as a projecting stone cornice. Construction of an L-shaped addition by architect Herman Lee Meader during 1920–22 maintained the building's original neoclassical character but, regrettably, destroyed the secondary elevations and the tower's original proportions.

**Cross Broadway and turn south. Stop at Wall Street to view the Empire Building, 71 Broadway, on the southeast corner of Rector Street.**

Francis H. Kimball was a leading designer of early skyscrapers, and several examples of his work are considered during this tour, including the **Empire Building**, 71 Broadway, built in 1895–96. (**4**) Many new office buildings were constructed in this area during the late nineteenth century, including Bradford Lee Gilbert's 11-story Tower Building of 1888–89, at 50 Broadway, just north of Bowling Green. Though it stood for only twenty-five years, it was the first tall building to incorporate a steel skeleton, making it the ancestor of nearly all skyscrapers. Kimball used similar technology in the Empire Building, which, like his nearby **Trinity Building**, at 111 Broadway, takes the shape of a narrow slab. (**5**) While the Trinity Building was designed in the neo-Gothic style during 1904–7, the 21-story Empire Building is in the Renaissance Revival style, with an eagle-flanked entry that suggests a Roman triumphal arch. The United States Steel Company, formed by Andrew Carnegie and later sold to JPMorgan & Company, purchased the structure in 1901 and used it as its headquarters until 1976. The building was converted to residential use in 1997.

**Turn east on Wall Street to the northeast corner of Broad Street.**

This famous intersection is closely connected to the history of American finance. Two of the buildings were designed by Trowbridge & Livingston: **23 Wall Street**, erected by J. P. Morgan at the southeast corner in 1913, (**6**) and the **Bankers Trust Building**, 14 Wall Street, located at the northwest corner, in 1910–12. (**7**) Designed in variants of the classical style, these buildings incorporate

The Bankers Trust Building of 1912 terminates in a stepped, pyramidal crown.

references to Greek, Roman, and Renaissance architecture. Like the American Surety Company, Bankers Trust was originally built as a freestanding tower, but during the early 1930s a restrained and complementary Art Deco–style addition—designed by the architects of the Empire State Building, Shreve, Lamb & Harmon—was wrapped around two sides. Try to imagine it standing all by itself, culminating in a monumental Ionic colonnade and a stepped stone pyramid that recalled the ancient Greek mausoleum of Halicarnassus. Sold in 1987, the spacious ground-story banking hall is now used as an athletic club.

## Continue east, stopping between Broad Street and William Street to view 37 Wall Street.

Clad in white marble and redbrick, the former **Trust Company of America** building is a handsome Beaux-Arts–style skyscraper that played a central role in the Panic of 1907. (**8**) For two weeks, depositors waited outside the building's entrance on Wall Street, withdrawing an estimated $14 million from the company. Though the company was bailed out by J. P. Morgan and others, people's fears led to reform and the eventual establishment of the Federal Reserve system. Built shortly before the crisis, in 1906–7, this sliver of a building was designed by Francis H. Kimball, and the multistory base is enlivened by prominent classical details, including plump putti and, over the entrance, the company's initials. Though almost lost as part of a plan to assemble a large site for a new New York Stock Exchange headquarters in the 1990s, 37 Wall Street has been spared and was recently converted to apartments. Directly across the street, at 40 Wall Street, is the former **Bank of Manhattan Company**. (**9**) H. Craig Severance (with Yasuo Matsui) was the architect and it was, briefly, the world's tallest building, surpassed by the Chrysler Building in 1930. (See pages 138, 139.)

## Continue east to the northeast corner of William Street to view 55 Wall Street.

Built by Boston architect Isaiah Rogers as the Merchants' Exchange in 1836–41 and later used as a U.S. Custom House, **55 Wall Street** was substantially enlarged by adding four stories and a Corinthian colonnade when it was acquired by National City Bank (now Citibank) in 1904. (**10**)

Though this is a difficult way for a building to grow, it works remarkably well and the addition is more or less seamless. At the time, the interiors were gutted and redesigned, creating one of the city's largest and most impressive banking halls, which today is leased for parties and special events. Designed by Charles F.

The former Merchants' Exchange, at 55 Wall Street, reflects two separate but surprisingly harmonious periods of construction.

McKim, of McKim, Mead & White, the vast interior has an impressive coffered ceiling and an immense dome decorated with astrological symbols. If the door is open and no event is under way, ask to take a glimpse inside.

**Continue east. Just before Hanover Street, enter 60 Wall Street and proceed through the public atrium, exiting to view 56 Pine Street.**

Louis Sullivan, the Chicago architect who celebrated the skyscraper in his writings and work, wrote in 1896 that the "tall office building . . . must be every inch a proud and soaring thing." Though **56 Pine Street** is only 12 stories tall, Sullivan certainly would have admired Oswald Wirz's 1894 design for the building, which stands between William and Pearl Streets. (11) Not only do the intricate carvings recall Sullivan's best work, but the facade has a strong vertical thrust, with relatively few horizontal interruptions. Clad with orange brick, sandstone, and terra-cotta, these marvelous carvings suggest Celtic, French medieval, and botanical sources.

**Turn west on Pine Street to William Street. Cross and ascend the raised plaza. Head west through the plaza, around Isamu Noguchi's *Sunken Garden* of 1964, to exit on Nassau Street and turn north, continuing to the southeast corner of Liberty Street to view Liberty Tower, at 55 Liberty Street.**

The public spaces that adjoin this spacious plaza provide a rare opportunity to step back and contemplate the character of the downtown skyline, with its stimulating jumble of twentieth-century styles, from Art Deco to the present day. The northwest corner is dominated by the **JPMorgan Chase Tower** of 1955–60 at 1 Chase Manhattan Plaza. (12) Recently, a great number of office buildings in lower Manhattan have been converted to apartments. **Liberty Tower** was the earliest of the group. (13) Architect Joseph Pell Lombardi, who lives on the 29th floor in the former boardroom of the Sinclair Oil Company, was responsible for the 1978 conversion. A beautiful example of the neo-Gothic style, it was built by architect Henry Ives Cobb in 1909–12. Clad entirely with terra-cotta, the steep white facades are embellished with crouching gargoyles and other details inspired by medieval church architecture. Such striking features may have influenced Cass Gilbert, who filed plans for his Woolworth Building the following year. (See pages 68, 69.)

Liberty Tower, at the corner of Nassau Street, is clad with white terra-cotta produced by the Atlantic Terra Cotta Company.

**Continue north and stop between Maiden Lane and John Street to view 63 Nassau Street.**

Tall buildings rely on industrial materials to achieve great height. Cast iron, introduced during the 1840s, contributed to the development of such buildings. Though the height of **63 Nassau Street** is low by contemporary standards, the iron used here was important because it was prefabricated and could be mass produced, streamlining the construction process. (14) (See page 42.) Also resistant to fire, from the 1850s to the 1880s it was widely used in commercial districts, especially in the areas now called SoHo and Ladies' Mile. This solitary iron-front building of 1857 was originally part of the jewelry district, making it one of the earliest in the city. It was designed by James Bogardus, who promoted the use of iron in architecture and is often called the "father" of cast-iron construction. Three stories tall, the painted facade displays small busts of Benjamin Franklin and George Washington, decorative features that Bogardus used in several other, now lost, works.

The Corbin Building, a narrow building facing Broadway and extending down John Street, was designed by skyscraper pioneer Francis H. Kimball in 1888–89.

**Continue north to John Street and turn west to the southeast corner of Broadway to view the Corbin Building at 11 John Street.**

Following the destruction of the World Trade Center, a new transit hub, designed by Grimshaw Architects, was planned for the east side of Broadway between John Street and Fulton Street. A group of buildings were razed to create the site, but the most significant one was saved: the **Corbin Building**. (**15**) (See page 41.) Constructed as a speculative venture in 1888–89, it was designed by Francis H. Kimball for banker-developer Austin Corbin, who helped consolidate the Long Island Railroad system. Situated on a narrow, trapezoidal site, a richly embellished eight-story facade stretches more than 160 feet along John Street. Above the brownstone base the decoration is particularly intricate, incorporating references to French Renaissance and medieval sources.

**The former headquarters of the American Telephone & Telegraph Company (AT&T) is located on the west side of Broadway, from John to Fulton Streets.**

Designed by William Wells Bosworth and built in several stages between 1910 and 1922, the former **headquarters of AT&T** is an austere and monumental piece of design, with three sets of stacked colonnades. (**16**) (See page 40.) Various types of classicism were popular before World War I, and this building has a decidedly Greek spirit, inspired by the temple of Artemis-Cybele in Sardis, Turkey (excavated between 1910 and 1914), and the Parthenon in Athens. Atop the west end of the building, near Church Street, a small pavilion is visible. Modeled on the mausoleum of Halicarnassus, like the Bankers Trust Building (see pages 54, 55), it is shaped like a stepped pyramid and once supported *Golden Boy*, a 40-ton gilt statue representing the "Genius of Electricity" by sculptor Evelyn Beatrice Longman. The building's marble lobby is particularly spectacular. Crowded with more than fifty Doric columns, it has an effect that is timeless and unforgettable. Reminiscent of great civic structures, this room suggests dependability and reliability—key characteristics for a corporation that was once the largest in the world.

**Turn north on Broadway. At Barclay Street, enter City Hall Park. Turn right at the fountain and exit onto Beekman Street. Continue one block east to the northeast corner of Beekman Street and Nassau Street.**

Though altered in 1902, the midsection of the **Morse Building**, 12 Beekman Street, on the northeast corner of Nassau and Beekman Streets, dates to 1878–80, making it one of Manhattan's oldest office buildings. (**17**) Though originally only ten stories tall, for a time it was the city's tallest. Built by Silliman & Farnsworth, it has an eclectic design, blending features associated with the Gothic, neo-Grec, and Romanesque Revival styles. Most of the floors display similar fenestration and brickwork, and little attempt was made by the architects to vary the

The former
American
Telephone &
Telegraph
Company
Building, with its
monumental
marble lobby,
was designated
a New York
City landmark
in 2006.

decoration or accentuate the building's height. Many early skyscrapers were designed in this manner, and the Morse Building is a rare survivor.

The **Temple Court Building**, 3-9 Beekman Street, stands directly across from the Morse Building at the southwest corner of Nassau Street and Beekman Street. (**18**) Designed by the same architects in 1881–83, it was named for the section of London where lawyers kept offices, and most of its early tenants were members of the legal profession. Like many buildings from this period, the aesthetic is eclectic, combining aspects of the neo-Grec, Gothic Revival, and Queen Anne styles. The twin peaked towers are Manhattan's earliest, anticipating the pairing of the nearby Trinity and United States Realty Buildings that flank Thames Street, and the glamorous uptown apartment buildings that line Central Park West, as well as the former World Trade Center towers. The annex, farther south along Nassau Street, was completed by Farnsworth in 1890.

**Continue north on Nassau Street. Cross Spruce Street and pause in the plaza that adjoins Pace University to view the former American Tract Society building, 150 Nassau Street, on the southeast corner of the intersection.**

The **American Tract Society**, a publisher of religious literature, built 150 Nassau Street in 1894–95. (**19**) R. H. Robertson, the designer of many fine churches in New York City, served as the architect. One of the earliest steel-frame skyscrapers in New York City, the building has steep brick and textured-granite elevations that were inspired by the work of H. H. Richardson and are embellished with Romanesque and Renaissance Revival features, such as triple-height arcades and a highly visible rooftop loggia supported by winged caryatids. Unfortunately, two elevator accidents in 1896 and 1897 made it difficult to attract tenants, and by 1914 the society (currently located in Texas) was unable to pay its mortgage. Subsequent tenants included the *New York Sun* and the *Evening Sun* newspapers. The 23-story building was converted to apartments in 2001.

**Proceed west along Spruce Street, crossing back to City Hall Park. Look across Park Row to view the Potter Building, 38 Park Row, and the former New York Times Building, 41 Park Row, between Spruce and Beekman Street.**

The **Potter Building**, 38 Park Row at the corner of Beekman Street, is among the most beautiful Victorian-era structures in Manhattan, recalling, though on a larger scale, buildings found in the South Kensington section of London. (**20**)

These two early skyscrapers were built as the offices and printing plants of the American Tract Society (left) and the *New York Times* (right).

Built in 1882–86, the red-and-black elevations incorporate brick, cast iron, and terra-cotta. First introduced in Massachusetts during the 1850s, terra-cotta did not gain wide popularity until the 1880s. Manufactured from burned clay, terra-cotta is a fireproof material that was frequently used as a substitute for more costly carved stone. The prominent brownish-red capitals that protect the columns and decorate the upper floors were produced by the Boston Terra Cotta Company. Orlando Potter, the real estate developer who commissioned the building, was so impressed with the results that he and the Boston firm's superintendent, James Taylor, organized the New York Architectural Terra Cotta Company in 1886, with offices and factory in Long Island City, Queens. Active for more than three decades, this company supplied terra-cotta for such landmarks as the Ansonia Hotel, at Broadway and 73rd Street, and the Montauk Club in Park Slope, Brooklyn.

To the north, at 41 Park Row, is the former **New York Times Building**, now part of Pace University. (**21**) During the newspaper's long history, the owners have built several memorable skyscrapers, including their current headquarters at 620 Eighth Avenue, between 40th and 41st Streets, designed by the Italian architect Renzo Piano. Their Romanesque Revival tower at 41 Park Row was designed by George B. Post in 1888–89 and was the company's last home in lower Manhattan. A student of Richard Morris Hunt, Post designed many important Manhattan buildings, including the New York Produce Exchange (demolished in the 1950s), the Brooklyn Historical Society, and the New York Stock Exchange. With the introduction of the telephone and subway, the *New York Times* decided to move north, following the *New York Herald*. Remarkably well preserved, 41 Park Row replaced an earlier *Times* building on the site, and reportedly the presses ran continuously as the new structure rose around and above it. The top four stories were added in 1903–5, following the paper's departure to midtown.

**Proceed south along Park Row, stopping between Beekman Street and Anne Street to view 15 Park Row.**

The world's tallest building may no longer be found in New York City, but many towers that once held the title can be found here. Less well known than subsequent title holders, the **Park Row Building**, 15 Park Row, designed by R. H. Robertson, certainly deserves attention. (**22**) Wide and somewhat flat, the 33-story Renaissance Revival–style structure was the world's tallest for almost a decade, from 1899 to 1908. The roof is crowned by a pair of circular domed

The principal facades of the redbrick Potter Building are
enlivened by sculpted terra-cotta ornament.

Twin observation pavilions rise from the roof of the Park Row Building, for nearly a decade the world's tallest office tower.

pavilions that originally served as public observation decks. Limestone figures by J. Massey Rhind, who produced a pair of bronze doors for Trinity Church and many other works, decorate the fourth story exterior.

**Continue circumambulating City Hall Park. Stop to view the Woolworth Building, 233 Broadway, between Barclay Street and Park Place.**

There are many reasons why the **Woolworth Building** is one of the most important early skyscrapers. (**23**) Completed in 1913, for sixteen years it was the world's tallest building, a 60-story tower that housed the offices of F. W. Woolworth's five-and-dime empire. Woolworth moved to New York City in 1886 and, before erecting a mansion on East 80th Street in Manhattan, lived in what is now called Bedford-Stuyvesant in a rather modest brownstone row house, commuting across the Brooklyn Bridge to his Manhattan office each day. It is, perhaps, for this reason that the Woolworth Building probably looks best from the bridge, where it can be compared to the other high-rise structures around it. Rising from a block-wide, 27-story podium, the slender massing of the splendid tower antic-

Nicknamed by critics the "Cathedral of Commerce," the Woolworth Building remains one of New York City's most memorable skyscrapers.

The neo-Gothic–style Woolworth Building has exquisitely detailed terra-cotta elevations. Though the predominant color scheme is white or cream, close observation reveals a range of colors, such as blue, green, and yellow.

ipates the setback zoning ordinance of 1916. Cass Gilbert, the building's architect, traveled with Woolworth in Europe, where they decided that the Gothic spires of late medieval France were the most appropriate model. Gilbert was a master of revival styles, and his earliest works were mainly neoclassical, such as the Beaux-Arts–style United States Custom House (now the National Museum of the American Indian and Federal Bankruptcy Court) on Bowling Green, followed by 90 West Street (at Cedar Street), his first skyscraper in the neo-Gothic idiom. Completion of the Woolworth Building, which stood almost 800 feet tall, was national news. President Woodrow Wilson, who was in Washington, DC, threw the switch that set the entire building aglow.

Large office buildings require many elevators to serve tenants and visitors. The Woolworth Building has one of the most spectacular rooms to house such necessities: a cruciform lobby decorated with a stained-glass ceiling, colorful murals of commerce and labor, and a glittery mosaic vault. Though access is now restricted, the base, as conceived by Gilbert, was permeable. One could enter the lobby not only from three streets but also through the adjoining shops and the subway station, which opened five years later in 1918. Part showpieces and part celebration, the elevators are flanked by whimsical plaster figures that represent the various men responsible for the building's creation—among others, Woolworth, Gilbert, engineer Gunwald Aus, and builder Louis J. Horowitz. Legend has it that Woolworth paid for his trophy with nothing but cash. Whether true or exaggerated, it was—and remains—one of the great buildings of the era.

**Continue north along the east side of Broadway to the corner of Murray Street to view the Home Life Insurance Company Building at 256 Broadway.**

The **Home Life Insurance Company Building** is another early steel-frame office building. (**24**) Constructed during 1892–94, this ornate Renaissance Revival tower, with a steep mansard roof and a marble facade, was designed by Pierre Le Brun of Napoleon Le Brun & Sons. Founded by Pierre's father in Philadelphia in the 1840s, the firm was responsible for nearly all the fire department buildings erected in Manhattan between 1870 and 1890. The firm also designed the Metropolitan Life Insurance Company Tower of 1909, inspired by the Campanile di San Marco in Venice, but at twice the scale. (See pages 116, 117.) The adjacent building at the corner of Murray Street, built for the Postal Telegraph Company, was acquired by Home Life in 1947.

Completed in 1915, the Municipal Building dominates views
from Brooklyn, the Brooklyn Bridge, and City Hall Park.

**Continue north to the northeast corner of Broadway and Chambers Street to view the Broadway-Chambers Building at 277 Broadway.**

Cass Gilbert was a Midwesterner who moved to New York City from St. Paul, Minnesota, in 1899. His first work in Manhattan, the **Broadway-Chambers Building**, is a vibrantly colored, 18-story office building with a brick facade, pink granite base, and ornate crown. (**25**) Though less well known than his subsequent buildings, Gilbert's distinguished design received an award at the Paris Exposition of 1900 and is a particularly successful example of a tripartite tower.

**Turn east to view the Municipal Building, at 1 Centre Street.**

By the early twentieth century, New York was a city of skyscrapers, and these office buildings had begun to overshadow the churches and residences of earlier times. In 1898 the five boroughs became Greater New York, and less than a decade later, in 1907, a public competition was held to design a structure that would house government offices and symbolize the city's new status and ambition. Though McKim, Mead & White rarely designed tall buildings, the neo-Renaissance style **Municipal Building** stands among the firm's finest works. (**26**) William M. Kendall, who joined the office in 1882, was chief designer. Built on an irregular hexagonal site, it was completed in 1915 and incorporates a triumphal arch that was planned as an extension to Chambers Street, a subway entrance arcade with handsome tiled vaults manufactured by the Guastavino Fireproof Construction Company, and a plaza screened by monumental Corinthian columns. One of the most prominent buildings on the downtown skyline, especially when seen from Brooklyn, the 500-foot-tall Municipal Building is crowned by a layered tower, with four turrets said to represent each of the boroughs, and a 25-foot-tall gilded statue by Adolph A. Weinman, symbolizing what all tall buildings aspire to: civic fame.

Leaving

**By Subway:** J, M, Z at Chambers Street; 4, 5, 6 at Brooklyn Bridge–City Hall
**By Bus:** M22, M15

## Suggested Reading

*Cass Gilbert, Architect*, by Sharon Irish. Monacelli Press, 1999. A biography of the architect who designed the Woolworth Building, the Broadway-Chambers Building, and many other exceptional works in the United States.

*Cast-Iron Architecture in America: The Significance of James Bogardus*, by Margot Gayle and Carol Gayle. W. W. Norton & Company, 1988. Margot Gayle founded the Friends of Cast-Iron Architecture in 1970. This organization played a central role in the designation of SoHo as an historic district in 1973, as well as raising public awareness of this important material. The biography sheds considerable light on Bogardus's career as an inventor and businessman and the critical role he played in pioneering the use of this material.

Landmarks Preservation Commission Reports. Most early skyscrapers discussed on this tour are designated New York City Landmarks, including the Morse Building and 195 Broadway. Recent reports prepared by my colleagues in the New York City Landmarks Preservation Commission's research department can be viewed at the agency's Web site: http://www.nyc.gov/html/lpc/html/forms/reports.shtml. Early designations, which tend to be much briefer, are available on the Neighborhood Preservation Center Web site: http://www.neighborhoodpreservationcenter.org /designation_reports.htm.

*The Rise of the New York Skyscraper, 1865–1913*, by Sarah Bradford Landau and Carl W. Condit. Yale University Press, 1996. Essential reading for scholars, students, and skyscraper fans.

*Terra-Cotta Skyline: New York's Architectural Ornament*, by Susan Tunick. New York: Princeton Architectural Press, 1997. No individual has done more to generate awareness of this architectural material than Susan Tunick. Beautifully illustrated with color photographs by Peter Mauss, it includes useful information on specific buildings and manufacturers.

# 3. Along the High Line

MATTHEW A. POSTAL

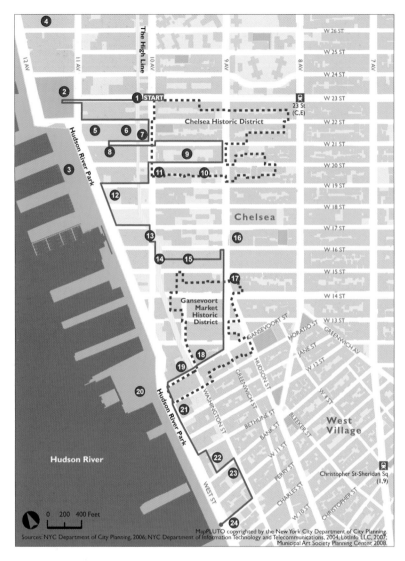

## Along the High Line

| | | |
|---|---|---|
| 1 the High Line | 10 Cushman Row | 19 end of the High Line |
| 2 Chelsea Waterside Park | 11 460 West 20th Street | 20 Pier 52 |
| 3 Chelsea Piers | 12 IAC Building | 21 former American Seamen's |
| 4 Starrett-Lehigh Building | 13 Tenth Avenue Square | Friend Society Home and |
| 5 former Dia Art Foundation | 14 Morimoto | Institute |
| space | 15 Chelsea Market | 22 Westbeth |
| 6 Comme des Garçons | 16 former National Maritime | 23 West Village Houses |
| 7 Guardian Angel Church | Union Building | 24 Richard Meier towers |
| 8 Paula Cooper Gallery | 17 Porter House | |
| 9 General Theological Seminary | 18 Florent | |

**By Subway:** C, E to 23rd Street
**By Bus:** M23

## Our tour begins at the southeast corner of Tenth Avenue and 23rd Street.

Look west to see the **High Line**, the last elevated railway built in Manhattan, where it spans 23rd Street on the far side of Tenth Avenue. (1) One and a half miles long, and 30 feet above the sidewalk, this steel viaduct originally served freight trains and connected the Penn Yards at 30th Street with St. John's Terminal, a massive two-story facility covering four entire blocks between Clarkson and Spring Streets. Completed in 1933, it was built by the New York Central Railroad, in partnership with the City of New York, as part of the West Side Improvement, which eliminated street-level railroad crossings along West Street, Eleventh Avenue, and Tenth Avenue. Related automobile projects included the nearby Miller Elevated Highway, remembered as the West Side Highway, which was demolished in stages between 1976 and 1989, and the Henry Hudson Parkway, built by Robert Moses and the State Parks Commission in the 1930s. Over the next four decades, activity on the High Line declined, and in 1980 the last delivery rumbled down the tracks. In subsequent years, the railbed stood quiet, attracting wildflowers and a steady flow of trespassers. While local property owners called for demolition, the Friends of the High Line, formed in 1999, persuaded the city council and the mayor to save the structure and convert it into a public park. This had been done with great success in Paris, where the former route of the Paris-Strasbourg railroad was transformed into a landscaped promenade in the twelfth arrondissement. In 2004, the Friends, and representatives from the City of New York, selected Field Operations and Diller Scofidio + Renfro, with planting designer Piet Oudulf, as the design team for the project. For those who supported the preservation and reuse of the High Line, this most unusual public park was a dramatic reversal, one that is transforming Manhattan's Lower West Side.

Rendering of High Line landscape.
Design by Field Operations and Diller Scofidio + Renfro. Courtesy the City of New York.

### Walk west on 23rd Street, crossing Eleventh Avenue into Chelsea Waterside Park.

Prior to World War II, access to the Hudson River was limited. Aside from Riverside Park and Battery Park, most of Manhattan's west side was devoted to mercantile use. A minor exception was Thomas F. Smith Park, located at the intersection of Eleventh Avenue and 23rd Street. In 1887, the Small Parks Law was passed, resulting in the creation of many new parks, chiefly in underserved tenement districts. Chelsea had many poor residents, and MAS played a role in the creation of Chelsea Park, located at Tenth Avenue between 27th and 28th Streets. This park, which was originally controlled by the Department of Docks, was trans-

ferred to the parks department in 1915 and, in 1923, was named for Smith, who served in the United States Congress. Expanded and renamed **Chelsea Waterside Park** in 2000, for many years it stood in the shadow of the West Side Highway. (2) Now controlled by the Hudson River Park Trust, it was designed by Thomas Balsley, the landscape architect of many waterfront spaces in New York City, most notably Gantry Park in Queens. The Hudson River Park will eventually extend from TriBeCa to 59th Street.

Two large structures are clearly visible from the park. To the south is **Chelsea Piers**, built in the 1900s to serve the Cunard and White Star Lines. (3) Extending from 17th Street to 22nd Street, the original stone-faced sheds were designed by Warren & Wetmore, architects of Grand Central Terminal. (See pages 158,

The netted golf driving range at Chelsea Piers is at the west end of 19th Street.

Completed in 1931, the Starrett-Lehigh Building is a superb example of streamlined modernism.

163.) For half a century it was a bustling gateway to New York, and many famous transatlantic passenger ships berthed at the 825-foot piers. Acquired by the city in the late 1950s and regrettably refaced with metal in 1963, the structures became a popular athletic facility—with a golf driving range, a swimming pool, and an ice-skating rink—in 1995.

To the north, at 601-625 West 26th Street, is the remarkable **Starrett-Lehigh Building**, completed in 1931. (**4**) Designed by Cory & Cory, with Yasuo Matsui as associate architect, this whale of a warehouse originally served as a freight terminal for the Lehigh Valley Railroad. Notable for its massive size and tiered brick elevations, it is a superb example of streamlined modernism. The stunning ribbon windows recall the work of the German architect Erich Mendelsohn, and it was one of a select group of local buildings included in the Museum of Modern Art's first architectural exhibition in 1932. Like the High Line, the Starrett-Lehigh Building was part of a multilevel urban vision in which rail and truck deliveries were seamlessly combined. Close to the railroad's 27th Street pier, the building had large elevators and concrete construction techniques that made it possible for heavy freight cars and trucks to enter and access any floor.

**Cross back to the east side of Eleventh Avenue and walk south to the northeast corner of 22nd Street to view 548 West 22nd Street.**

Chelsea is now New York City's premier gallery district. A key player in the neighborhood's transformation was the **Dia Art Foundation**, which moved to 548 West 22nd Street in 1990. (**5**) Though Dia is now closed, the long-term exhibitions that it mounted in this location helped put Chelsea on the map, and many commercial galleries gathered in the vicinity, initially along 22nd and 24th Streets and now as far north as 30th Street. Dia was also responsible for the trees and basalt rocks that line both sidewalks. They are part of a permanent installation created by the German artist Joseph Beuys, titled *7000 Oaks*, which debuted at Documenta 7 in Kassel, Germany, in 1982. This quiet work reflects the artist's lifelong engagement with social and environmental concerns.

**Walk east along the north side of 22nd Street and pause midblock at 520 West 22nd Street.**

Before passing beneath the High Line, stop to consider the shop **Comme des Garçons**. (**6**) Located in a late nineteenth-century brick warehouse and marked only by a sign for the previous tenant, Heavenly Body Works, one enters the store through a curving aluminum tube designed by the innovative British firm Future Systems. Swing open the oval glass door, pass through the tube, and enter an exquisite retail space. Japanese designer Rei Kawakubo founded Comme des Garçons in Tokyo in 1973 and opened this Chelsea showroom in 1999. To design the interior, she collaborated with the architect Takao Kawasaki, as well as Studio Morsa. White enamel blankets the modular shelving units that stand throughout the room. Meticulously crafted in Japan, they gently bend and turn, recalling pieces of abstract sculpture. Minimal and somewhat austere, this elegant space is the perfect foil for Kawakubo's fashionable and expensive clothing.

**Continue east to the corner of Tenth Avenue, then turn south to the northwest corner of 21st Street.**

The High Line was one of the largest eminent-domain projects of its day. To create an off-street, midblock path took several hundred real estate transactions, though in only a dozen cases was condemnation required. One example is the **Guardian Angel Church**, at 193 Tenth Avenue. (**7**) Originally located on 23rd Street, the Roman Catholic congregation agreed to sell its property in 1930. A substantial parcel was acquired on Tenth Avenue, extending north from the corner of 21st Street. John V. Van Pelt was commissioned to design the new complex, which includes a church, rectory, and school. Trained at the École des Beaux-Arts in Paris, he designed many churches, taught at Columbia University, and served as dean of the College of Architecture at Cornell University. Though Van Pelt once described the Gothic style as "the only style that can architecturally express religious emotion," for this project he looked to the Romanesque period. Some writers have suggested a relation to southern Sicilian models, from where members of the congregation may have come, but the ornate portal and lavish limestone detail seem inspired by French medieval sources. Inside the church, stained-glass windows by F. X. Zettler of Munich display images of a ship and anchor. In the late 1930s the congregation's pastor also served as the archdiocese's port chaplain.

**Walk west along 21st Street and pause midblock to view 534 West 21st Street.**

**Paula Cooper Gallery**, SoHo's first, opened on Prince Street in 1968. When she relocated to 534 West 21st Street in 1996, it was a momentous event, signaling the end of an era. **(8)** West Chelsea feels a bit like Los Angeles, and art dealers are attracted to the quiet, low-rise streets where vacant industrial structures can be converted easily into white-walled galleries. Cooper's space, located in a midblock warehouse, has a rustic Zen-like elegance that feels right with the minimalist artists she favors. It was designed by Richard Gluckman of Gluckman Mayner, arguably Chelsea's most popular architect, having designed Dia in 1987–89 as well as a handful of other prestigious galleries, including Mary Boone (541 West 24th Street) and Cheim & Reid (547 West 25th Street). Admired for his light touch and his sensitivity to natural light, he preserved much of the building's original texture and fabric, including the dark timber ceiling that floats above the main room.

**Return east along 21st Street to the northeast corner of Tenth Avenue.**

Crossing Tenth Avenue, once referred to as "Death Alley" due to the large number of accidents caused by freight trains, you enter the Chelsea Historic District. Situated along the east side of Tenth Avenue, it extends irregularly from 20th to 23rd Streets. Clement Clarke Moore, a writer and theologian associated with Trinity Church and St. Luke's Chapel, inherited much of the area in 1813, and during the 1830s, with the help of carpenter and builder James N. Wells, he began to develop it. They divided the property into building lots, and restrictive covenants were used to guide the character of future construction. Unlike most early nineteenth-century New York neighborhoods, there would be no alleys, stables, or back houses. At the center of the development, along the south side of 21st Street, an entire block was set aside for the **General Theological Seminary**. (**9**) Founded in 1817, the seminary occupies the block bordered by Ninth Avenue, Tenth Avenue, 21st Street, and 20th Street. The Episcopal school offers graduate programs in theology and has recently established the Desmond Tutu Education Center, named for the Nobel Prize–winning South African theologian, at the west end of campus. While the earliest structure on the campus dates from 1836, most of the brick and brownstone buildings were designed according to the master plan of 1883, prepared by the architect Charles Coolidge Haight. At the center of the block is the Chapel of the Good Shepherd. Designed in the Collegiate Gothic style by Haight in 1885–88, it dominates the seminary with a 160-foot-tall bell tower and bronze doors designed by the sculptor J. Massey Rhind. (See also page 52–54.) The campus, considered the oldest in the city, can be visited. Request permission at 175 Ninth Avenue, or view the lush grounds through the iron fence that runs along the north side of 20th Street.

**Continue east to Ninth Avenue, turn south for one block, and turn west onto 20th Street to view Cushman Row, 406-418 West 20th Street.**

Opposite the chapel stands **Cushman Row**, a group of some of the finest Greek Revival houses in Manhattan. (**10**) The dry-goods merchant Don Alonzo Cushman moved to Chelsea in 1830 and became an important developer in the area. He was a close friend of Clement Clarke Moore, and both worshipped at Trinity Church. (See page 49.) The well-preserved four-story brick houses at 406-418 West 20th Street were built in 1839–40. Set behind deep generous gardens, these elegant residences display much of their original ironwork and wood detailing. In addition to the houses Cushman built at 355-361 West 20th Street, Cush-

Cushman Row's Greek Revival townhouses were developed by dry-goods merchant Don Alonzo Cushman in 1839–40.

man's heirs also built the Donac, an apartment building with an unusual curved facade at 402 West 20th Street.

**Continue west on 20th Street and stop at the northwest corner of Tenth Avenue to view 460 West 20th Street.**

When west Chelsea was designated an historic district in 1970 (and expanded in 1981), the Landmarks Preservation Commission chose to include a gasoline station at the southeast corner of Tenth Avenue and 20th Street. Though the building did not have much architectural significance, the commission's decision allowed it to remain involved with the site and to judge how future construction might affect the adjoining residential buildings. Richard Cook, of Cook+Fox Architects, designed the building that replaced the gas station, the Chelsea Grande apartment house at **460 West 20th Street**, completed in 2004. (11) Cook has been responsible for many successful preservation projects in Manhattan, most notably historic Front Street, completed in 2006, where he cleverly inserted new structures into a block of seriously deteriorated buildings in the South Street Seaport Historic District. What resulted in Chelsea is similar: an uncommonly good neighbor with interesting contemporary details. Faced with iron-spot brick, masonry, and painted metalwork, the building has a distinctive pair of elevations that incorporate subtle references to both the district and the High Line.

**Turn south one block to 19th Street and then walk west to the corner of Eleventh Avenue.**

Best viewed from West Street or, most likely, from a boat floating on the Hudson, the **IAC Building** of 2007 is Frank Gehry's first completed work in New York City. (12) Prior to this commission, the celebrated Los Angeles architect had completed only two projects here: the striking but private Condé Nast cafeteria of 2002 and a titanium sculpture for the Issey Miyake store in TriBeCa. Located near the south end of Chelsea Piers, on a site previously occupied by truck garages, the nine-story archi-sculpture has a curtain wall of smoky white glass and stands 155 feet tall. The billowing, tiered forms have been compared to windswept sails morphing into an Art Deco period spire—a fitting tribute to the city's harbor and skyline. It is an excellent location for this type of design, allowing us to see it from afar and on three sides. To appreciate Gehry's aesthetic fully, stroll around the building to 18th Street, cross West Street carefully, and view it from multiple angles.

Facing the Hudson River and Eleventh Avenue, the IAC Building was the first structure in New York City designed by Frank Gehry.

**Turn south on Eleventh Avenue to 17th Street and then walk east to Tenth Avenue. Turn south again and look up to view Tenth Avenue Square, between 16th and 17th Streets. (13)**

Between 30th Street and 19th Street, the High Line advances in a straight line, shooting between the various midblock commercial buildings it once served. Near 18th Street, however, the track turns and divides, with one section heading toward the 1920s cold-storage building on the west side of Tenth Avenue and the other veering east. Stand alongside the yellow brick building, looking south, to view where the tracks emerge and then join together. At 16th Street, the High Line enters the former Nabisco factory, now Chelsea Market. Constructed in stages between 1890 and 1932, the last addition to the 22-building complex was designed so that freight trains could enter and pass through the building. This unique feature, one of only two examples that remain along the tracks, is certain to be one of the park's more memorable spots. Not only will the public be pro-

The west section of the former Nabisco factory, now Chelsea Market, was rebuilt in 1932 to accommodate the path of the High Line.

tected from the elements, but at 15th Street the elevated terrace will provide breathtaking views of the Hudson River and beyond.

**Cross to the east side of the street and proceed south, stopping midblock between 16th and 15th Streets.**

Beneath the tracks is **Morimoto**, 88 Tenth Avenue, a restaurant designed by the renowned Japanese architect Tadao Ando in 2005–6. (**14**) Restaurateur Steven Starr, who began his career in the entertainment field and has ten restaurants in Philadelphia, certainly knows how to generate buzz. Not only did he commission Ando's first work in New York City, but simultaneously he opened Buddakan around the corner at 75 Ninth Avenue, an Asian restaurant with highly theatrical interiors by the French interior designer Christian Liagre. Morimoto is entered through a galvanized steel arch shrouded in red curtains. Inside there is plenty of the architect's trademark concrete, visible in a row of 14 freestanding pillars, but the overall effect is softened by a two-story-high wall of glass water bottles and a ceiling draped in luminous fiberglass. Though hardly comparable to Ando's most celebrated works, such as the serene churches and museums he designed in Japan, Morimoto is, nonetheless, an ethereal space that deserves a visit.

## Just south of Morimoto, enter Chelsea Market.

**Chelsea Market** now occupies the former Nabisco factory, in its heyday the largest factory in Chelsea, covering 46 acres. (**15**) Many popular sweets were produced here, including the Oreo, introduced in 1912. The plant closed in 1958 and, after serving various industrial tenants, was acquired by a group of investors led by Irwin B. Cohen, an imaginative developer who frequently works with artists to enliven vacant industrial space. An earlier project in Long Island City had led to an important legal case. Using broken tile, scrap metal, and other industrial detritus, the artists known as the "Three Js" transformed the corridor of a former Macy's warehouse into what one critic called a "scrap yard wonderland." The subsequent owner, however, did not appreciate their unusual work and developed plans to dismantle it. The artists, as well as MAS, which organized frequent public visits to the site, maintained that their environment deserved full protection under the Visual Artists Act of 1991. The U.S. Court of Appeals, nonetheless, sided with the owner in 2002, and much of the installation, including the wall sculptures, floor mosaics, and whimsical elevators, has since been compromised.

Chelsea Market's shopping concourse features various works of art, including this gushing fountain, made from recycled materials.

An imaginative form of adaptive reuse, Chelsea Market has become a favorite destination for amateur cooks and professional chefs.

At Chelsea Market, however, the story is much sunnier. For this project, Cohen hired the architect Jeff J. Vandeberg to create an 800-foot-long concourse linking Ninth and Tenth Avenues. While the glass-and-aluminum storefronts are modern and unassuming, the corridor retains a gritty sense of mystery, punctuated by blasted brick arches, walls lined with recycled light posts and granite reliefs by sculptor Mark Mennin, and a powerful waterfall that gushes from a cast-iron pipe. A wonderful place to shop and eat, the market contains food manufacturers and distributors, including shops devoted to baked goods, soups, vegetables, and Italian delicacies. This unorthodox approach has given the former bakery cachet, and many of the upper floors are now leased to media companies, including, most appropriately, the Food Network.

**Proceed through Chelsea Market to the exit at Ninth Avenue. Turn north to the corner of 16th Street and view the Maritime Hotel on the opposite side of the avenue.**

In the mid-1960s, the **National Maritime Union** built two unconventional buildings: its headquarters on Seventh Avenue, between 12th and 13th Streets, and an L-shaped training facility and dorm at the corner of Ninth Avenue and 17th Street. (**16**) Both structures were designed by Albert C. Ledner, a New Orleans architect who studied with Frank Lloyd Wright. While the Seventh Avenue building (now an annex of St. Vincent's Hospital) displays unusual scallop-shaped setbacks that recall Wright's Marin County Building, the latter building is distinguished by sloping facades and porthole-like windows. Both were named to honor Joseph Curran, the union's Manhattan-born founder and former deckhand who established the organization in 1936 and served as its president until 1973. These structures, however, were poorly timed. With local shipping activity and union membership in steady decline, the building was sold in 1987 and subsequently divided into separate structures. Fortunately, the Ninth Avenue wing attracted a sympathetic buyer and has been successfully converted by the developers Sean MacPherson and Eric Goode into a fashionable hotel with a nautical spirit. Though the plaza has been elevated and is now occupied by restaurants, the unusual facade has been retained, and a salty air remains. Not only do the outdoor spaces recall the deck of an ocean liner, but the blue-toned lobby, entered from 363 West 17th Street, features a charming frieze of ships in the harbor.

**Return south on Ninth Avenue to 15th Street and view the Porter House apartments, 66 Ninth Avenue, on the southeast corner.**

Built as a dorm for the National Maritime Union in 1966, this quirky concrete structure is now the Maritime Hotel.

The **Porter House** rises at the north end of the meatpacking district. (**17**) Aptly named for a prime cut of steak, this apartment house is a curious marriage of past and present. Designed by Greg Pasquarelli of SHoP Architects in 2003, it juxtaposes two distinct architectural forms: a six-story brick warehouse built for a wine importer in 1905 and a four-story addition that cantilevers slightly above

The Porter House, a cantilevered apartment building at the corner of Ninth Avenue and 15th Street.

a group of 1840s houses to the south. Faced in zinc, glass, and internally mounted light boxes that can be illuminated after dark, this striking building recalls the late work of Jean Prouvé and other French architects of the 1970s.

## Continue south on Ninth Avenue to the intersection of Gansevoort Street.

How quickly Manhattan neighborhoods change! The Gansevoort Historic District extends roughly from Gansevoort Street to 14th Street between Hudson and Washington Streets. It is situated where the irregular street pattern of the colonial era intersects with the modern gridiron, first proposed in 1811. Since the mid-nineteenth century, local farmers have gathered in the area to sell produce first in open stalls and later in purpose-built structures. Meat slowly began to dominate sales, and in 1949 the Gansevoort Meat Center was erected with public funds at the southeast corner of Tenth Avenue and Washington Street. In 2003, the Landmarks Preservation Commission designated much of the surrounding neighborhood as an historic district. While designation protects specific physical features—such as the granite block streets, wood and metal awnings, and most structures—it will not slow the inevitable exodus of the meatpacking industry to less-expensive neighborhoods.

**Turn west on Gansevoort Street and walk to number 69.**

Gansevoort Street between Ninth Avenue and Washington Street is one of the neighborhood's most distinctive blocks. Among the businesses that line both sides of Gansevoort Street, the former R & L Restaurant has one of the most distinctive storefronts. Clad in gleaming stainless steel, this working-class diner later became **Florent**, an open-all-hours restaurant known for its solid French bistro fare and for being a neighborhood pioneer. (**18**) Founded at a time when few New Yorkers ventured into the meatpacking district, owner Florent Morellet became a neighborhood fixture and later organized the Save the Gansevoort

The sleek facade of the R&L Restaurant, later Florent, then changed back to its original name in 2008, dates from the period when Gansevoort Street was the heart of the meatpacking district.

Rendering of Gansevoort Street entry, looking north.
Design by Field Operations and Diller Scofidio + Renfro. Courtesy the City of New York.

Market group in 1999, which led to the area's historic designation. Escalating rents, however, threatened the popular restaurant, and Morellet closed his restaurant on June 29, 2008.

### Continue west to the northeast corner of Washington Street to view the end of the High Line.

Where Gansevoort Street intersects with Washington Street, the **High Line** ends or, depending on your point of view, begins. (**19**) Construction began in April 2006, and this corner will eventually serve as the park's south entrance. The tracks beyond Gansevoort Street were demolished in two stages, below Bank Street in 1963 and south of where you stand in 1991. Despite the loss, traces of the original route can be discerned along the west side of Washington Street. Bricked-up walls reveal clues, but also examine the way in which some buildings are massed to suggest where the trains once traveled.

**Continue west on Gansevoort Street to Tenth Avenue, looking toward the Hudson River.**

At the west end of Gansevoort Street is **Pier 52**, the former site of a warehouse operated by the Baltimore and Ohio Railroad. (**20**) It was here, in this unlikely location, that the daring sculptor and conceptual artist Gordon Matta-Clark created *Day's End* (also known as *Day's Passing*) in the summer of 1975. With much of the waterfront quiet and abandoned, he took over the vacant warehouse and created one of his most provocative and satisfying works: a series of circular cuts in thick steel walls and wood supports that transformed the immense interior into a shimmering, light-filled space. At the west end of the building, facing the river and New Jersey, was the largest cut, a crescent-shaped aperture that admitted direct light in the late afternoon. Like most of the artist's so-called cuttings, *Day's End* was temporary and today is known only through films and photographs.

**Turn south. At Horatio Street, Tenth Avenue becomes West Street. Continue south to the corner of Jane Street to view 505–507 West Street.**

505–507 West Street is a century-old brick structure that once housed the **American Seamen's Friend Society Home and Institute**. (**21**) Founded in 1826 to "improve the social and moral condition of seamen," the society operated boarding houses along the Manhattan waterfront, as well as small libraries on ships. This structure, which originally housed a chapel, a concert hall, and a bowling alley, was funded by Olivia Sage, widow of the financier Russell Sage and one of the city's great philanthropists. William A. Boring, who codesigned many of the structures on Ellis Island, served as architect. Completed in 1910, the building's most famous guests were the surviving crew of the ill-fated *Titanic* who were brought here to recuperate in April 1912. Since 1944, under various names, the building has been a residential hotel.

**Continue south on West Street to the corner of Bethune Street.**

**Westbeth** rises at Bethune Street, a full-block complex of eight industrial buildings constructed for the Western Electric Company, later known as Bell Telephone Laboratories. (**22**) This firm pioneered many technological breakthroughs during the twentieth century, including the invention of the transistor. The oldest structure, located one block south at the corner of West and Bank Streets, dates

View of the courtyard at Westbeth, an early work by Richard Meier.

to the period of the Civil War. The latest structure, built to the east along Washington Street by McKenzie, Voorhees & Gmelin in 1923–26, was altered in 1931–34 to permit the High Line to pass through. The lab shut down in 1966, and the complex has been converted into artists' housing. The J. M. Kaplan Fund, which helped save Carnegie Hall and launched the MAS bookstore, Urban Center Books, provided the necessary seed money, along with the National Endowment for the Arts. Completed in 1970, Westbeth was described by the *New York Times* as the "world's largest housing project for artists." The complex was also the architect Richard Meier's first major commission in New York City. Loosely inspired by Le Corbusier's Unité d'Habitation in Marseille, France, Westbeth combines apartments, commercial spaces, and community facilities. To create a series of public spaces, a small group of low-rise structures was removed, opening a tiered plaza to the south, through-block passages, and a narrow central courtyard. This semienclosed space incorporates the types of modern flourishes we associate with Meier, including a switchback ramp and rows of curved white metal balconies.

**To view the courtyard, turn east onto Bethune Street and ascend the stairs on the right. Exit to the south, passing through the wide plaza on Bank Street. Stop to view the West Village Houses, located on the south side of Bank Street, extending east from the middle of the block to the corner of Washington Street.**

Built in the mid-1970s, the **West Village Houses**—simple six-story apartment buildings—were the first structures constructed to replace the High Line. (23) Though early proposals called for apartment towers, opposition from local residents, including the author Jane Jacobs, who lived nearby at 555 Hudson Street, led to the present configuration. Completed in stages, the 42 buildings (interspersed with gardens) are arranged irregularly along the west side of Washington Street, as far south as Morton Street, as well as on some of the side streets that lead to the river. Designed by J. Raymond Matz of Perkins & Will, these brick-and-concrete structures are notable less for their aesthetic character, which tries to merge the brownstone tradition with Brutalism, and more for their human scale, front stoops, and lack of elevators—features that Jacobs maintained would encourage frequent and unplanned social contact between tenants. Though conceived as middle-class cooperatives, few units sold, and by 1975 the city-owned apartments became rentals. In recent years, however, steps have been successfully taken by residents to convert the buildings to cooperative ownership.

Built in two campaigns, between 2002 and 2006, these striking glass apartment towers were also designed by Richard Meier.

**At the corner of Bank Street and Washington Street, turn south and proceed two blocks to Perry Street. Turn west and proceed to the end of the block, cross the highway, and enter Hudson River Park.**

A tree-lined boulevard with modest landscaping, this is the first completed section of Hudson River Park. Completed in 2001 and designed by Thomas Balsley Associates, it is a pleasure to visit, incorporating three peaceful piers, a grassy esplanade, and, near Jane Street, a delightful children's water playground with a maritime theme. Though considerably less ambitious (and expensive) than the controversial Westway project of the 1970s, which proposed to bury the adjoining roadway, the park is satisfying and the views are remarkable. Hudson River Park has spurred a massive redevelopment of the adjoining blocks in Greenwich Village. Among the various buildings constructed between Washington and West

Streets since the demise of the High Line, **three glass towers** by Richard Meier stand out. **(24)** The architect Richard Meier, who is based in New York City, has produced buildings throughout the world but, except for the adaptive reuse of Westbeth, nothing other than private interiors in Manhattan. Built for a consortium of developers, the first pair of 15-story towers, straddling the west end of Perry Street, was completed in 2002, and 165 Charles Street, the largest of the three, opened in 2006. Serene and modern, they are comparable to the black steel apartment towers Mies van der Rohe designed overlooking Lake Michigan in Chicago during 1948–51. Though different in terms of color and details, these striking buildings demonstrate the continuing appeal of industrial materials and the aesthetic of transparency. Set behind small, raised, granite plazas, the facades are beautifully articulated, incorporating white aluminum screens that frame and slide across the bluish-green glass walls and terraces. Despite their obvious architectural quality, these luxury buildings have generated considerable controversy. Community groups rightly fear what will follow, and many new apartment houses—most likely of similar dimensions but of less architectural interest—are planned. As much as any building on Manhattan's lower west side, the Meier towers symbolize how New York and its waterfront have changed.

Leaving

**By Subway:** 1 at Christopher Street–Sheridan Square
**By Bus:** M20

## Suggested Reading

*Gansevoort Market Historic District Designation Report*, by Jay Shockley. Landmarks Preservation Commission, 2003. This in-depth study examines the neighborhood from its origins as a public food market to the present day.

*The New York Waterfront: Evolution and Building Culture of the Port and Harbor*, edited by Kevin Bone. Monacelli Press, 2003. A fascinating history of the once-forgotten Hudson and East River waterfronts, with essays by Mary Beth Betts, Eugenia Bone, Gina Pollard, and Donald Squiers.

*Reclaiming the High Line*, by Joshua David. Design Trust for Public Space, 2002. Together with Robert Hammond, Joshua David formed the Friends of the High Line in 1999. This well-timed publication provided an invaluable history of the High Line and a preliminary blueprint for its eventual reuse.

*Turn West on 23rd: A Toast to New York's Old Chelsea*, by Robert Baral. Fleet Publishing Corporation, 1965. This chatty, anecdotal history of the area focuses mostly on the residential blocks east of Tenth Avenue and particularly concerns events associated with the Hotel Chelsea, the Grand Opera House, and Clement Clarke Moore.

# 4. Of Farragut and Flatiron

## FRANCIS MORRONE

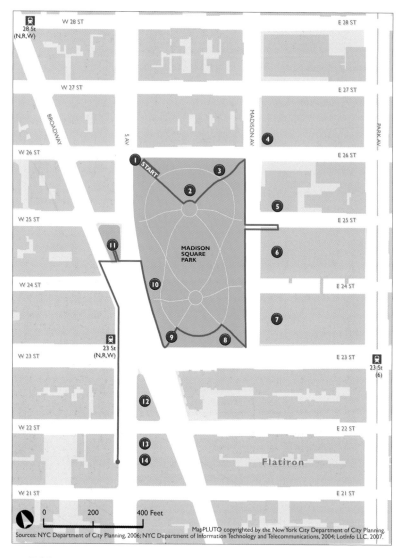

## Of Farragut and Flatiron

1   overview of Madison Square
2   Admiral David Glasgow Farragut monument
3   Chester A. Arthur statue
4   New York Life Insurance Company Building
5   New York State Supreme Court, Appellate Division
6   former north annex of the Metropolitan Life Insurance Company
7   former headquarters of the Metropolitan Life Insurance Company
8   Roscoe Conkling statue
9   William H. Seward statue
10  Eternal Light Monument
11  Worth Monument
12  Flatiron Building
13  former Glenham Hotel
14  Rapaport House of United Synagogues of America

**By Subway:** N, R, W to 28th Street
**By Bus:** M2, M3, M5, M6, M7

## Begin at the southeast corner of Fifth Avenue and 26th Street.

**M**adison Square is what remains of a large open space, bounded by Third and Seventh Avenues and 23rd and 34th Streets, indicated on the Commissioners' Plan of 1811 and labeled the "Grand Parade"— which is a fancier way of saying "Central Park." (1) In other words, De Witt Clinton's commissioners thought that maybe this would be the right setting for a metropolitan greensward. The uptown growth of the city, however, was so rapid, and the desirability for residential purposes of this part of the island so great, that the Grand Parade was whittled down to Madison Square, which was landscaped in the 1840s when fine houses began going up in a neighborhood that soon became a bastion of the city's elite—for example, Theodore Roosevelt grew up on 20th Street between Broadway and Park Avenue South, and Edith Wharton on 23rd Street between Fifth and Sixth Avenues. Delmonico's, the city's most legendary restaurant and host to the Patriarchs' Balls and debutante balls, was on Fifth Avenue at the southwest corner of 26th Street from 1876 to 1899. In this neighborhood once lived the characters that populated novels by Edith Wharton. Madison Square—like Union Square, Gramercy Park, and Washington Square—was an elegant residential square. Little sense of that remains today. By the end of the nineteenth century, stores, theaters, hotels, and office buildings had begun to transform the neighborhood. Though the area's early commercial days were quite upmarket, in time this became a little-thought-of precinct of wholesale jobbers and craft-trades workshops. Around 1970 or so it might have been difficult to imag-

The monument to Admiral David Glasgow Farragut, with a bronze statue by Augustus Saint-Gaudens and an exedra by Saint-Gaudens and Stanford White, was recognized early as one of the most important public artworks in America.

ine that the neighborhood would regain its onetime luster and that, just as in the days of Delmonico's, New Yorkers would flock to Madison Square—or its greater environs christened the "Flatiron District"—to dine at some of the city's chicest eateries. But we should never be surprised by such things, as it is in the nature of cities that they are resilient.

**Enter the park walking southeast along the diagonal pathway and stop at the fountain directly ahead.**

Here in the north central part of the square is a modern fountain installed by the public-private partnership that around 2000 undertook an extensive renovation of what had become a dilapidated square. Facing the fountain from the north is one of the most prized works of public art in New York: the monument to **Admiral David Glasgow Farragut**. (2) The bronze standing figure of the Civil War admiral is a study in fortitude. The face shows a resoluteness that stands in comparison with Holbein's celebrated portrait of Sir Thomas More in the Frick Collection. The Farragut Monument, begun in 1876 and dedicated on March 25,

1881, was the first public commission granted to Augustus Saint-Gaudens, one of the greatest American sculptors of all time. New York is blessed in having Saint-Gaudens's first public work and also one of his last, the General Sherman Monument at Fifth Avenue and 59th Street. Both are among the masterpieces of American art. A further fascination of the Farragut Monument is its stone exedra. (An exedra is a sculptural base that is also a bench. Go ahead—sit on it. You're meant to!) It was designed by Saint-Gaudens together with his friend, a young architect named Stanford White, who at the time was not yet a member of the firm of McKim, Mead & White. Note the sinuous marine motifs flanked by personifications of Loyalty and Courage, and the stylized lettering of texts relating aspects of Farragut's career. The texts were prepared by Richard Grant White, one of nineteenth-century New York's leading men of letters as well as the father of Stanford White. In the pebbled foreground of the exedra is a bronze crab inscribed with the names of Saint-Gaudens and Stanford White. The handsome monument was restored in 2002 under the MAS Adopt-a-Monument program.

New York is blessed to have the best of both the early and the late phases of the career of America's greatest sculptor. Here is Augustus Saint-Gaudens's General Sherman Monument on Fifth Avenue at 59th Street, from 1903.

Chester Alan Arthur, twenty-first president of the United States, lived near here on Lexington Avenue at 28th Street. The statue of him, by George Edwin Bissell, is said to be an exacting likeness.

**Continue northeast along the diagonal path toward the corner of 26th Street and Madison Avenue.**

View a bronze statue of **Chester A. Arthur**, the twenty-first president of the United States and a longtime New York City resident. (**3**) The sculptor, George Edwin Bissell, was among his generation's most accurate portraitists. The statue was dedicated in 1899.

**Continue to the path's end at 26th Street and Madison Avenue to view the New York Life Insurance Company Building on the northeast corner of the intersection.**

The **New York Life Insurance Company Building** (1926), 51 Madison Avenue, is one of the undersung beauties of New York architecture. (**4**) Architecture buffs are acutely aware that this building replaced Stanford White's exquisite Madison Square Garden. Cass Gilbert, the architect of the New York Life Building, had once worked for McKim, Mead & White before moving to St. Paul, Minnesota, where he designed the state capitol. In 1899 Gilbert returned to New York, for good, when he won the competition for the United States Custom House at Bowling Green. The New York Life Building, like Madison Square Garden before it, occupies an entire square block. Gilbert's skyscraper steps back as it rises, its masses outlined in delicate ornamental tracery, to a golden pyramidal crown that since 1926 has been the symbol of the onetime largest insurance company in America. The true grandeur of the building, however, lies within, in the majestic, barrel-vaulted through-block lobby, one of the finest interiors in New York, with murals by Ezra Winter. You can no longer freely traverse the length of the lobby, which is sad, but the guard on a good day may let you stand inside the doorway for an awed look down the great hall.

**Turn south on Madison Avenue to 25th Street. Cross the avenue to view the facade of the courthouse of the Appellate Division of the New York State Supreme Court on the north side of the street.**

One of New York's greatest buildings, the courthouse of the **Appellate Division of the New York State Supreme Court**, 35 East 25th Street, opened in

Cass Gilbert designed the headquarters of New York Life Insurance on the site of the first two iterations of Madison Square Garden, including the one designed by Stanford White. Topped by a gold pyramid, the New York Life Building is one of New York's most beautiful skyscrapers.

The Appellate Division Courthouse, designed by James Brown Lord, features one of the most beautiful pediments in New York, filled, as pediments are meant to be, with figure sculpture. The crowning group is *Justice* by Daniel Chester French.

1900. (**5**) The architect, James Brown Lord, hailed from two distinguished New York families: the Browns (of Brown Brothers) and the Lords (of the famous law firm, no longer in existence, of Lord, Day & Lord). He had also, like Cass Gilbert, once worked for McKim, Mead & White. This is perhaps the truest "Palladian" building in New York, for unlike other buildings putatively in the idiom of the High Renaissance master Andrea Palladio, the courthouse features opulent exterior decoration just as do Palladio's own works in the Veneto. Flanking the front stairs, on 25th Street, are seated figures in stone, *Force* and *Wisdom*, by Frederick Wellington Ruckstull. The raking cornices of the triangular pediment properly frame sculptural imagery, in this case symbols of the law. The artist was the German-born Charles Henry Niehaus, who produced some of this country's finest architectural sculpture. Too often in New York, especially in the so-called Greek Revival of the early nineteenth century, our architects left the space within the pediment bare. It is like going to a museum and seeing fine frames with no pictures in them. Not so at this courthouse.

Most noteworthy are the standing figures, in stone, arrayed along the building's attic, the bodies etched against the sky, demonstrating how architecture and sculpture can work hand in hand for an aesthetic effect of a kind neither art form can achieve purely on its own. These figures are meant to be appraised and identified by the viewer of the building. They are of great lawgivers and lawmakers through history. From left to right along 25th Street we see figures of Zoroaster (Persian law), Alfred the Great (Saxon law), Lycurgus (Spartan law), and Solon (Athenian law). Then we see an elaborate central group, *Justice*, by Daniel Chester French. Then follow Louis IX (French law), the mythological Manu (Indian law), and

The narrow side of the Appellate Division Courthouse faces Madison Square, and so was as painstakingly detailed as the main facade on 25th Street. The central group at the top is *Peace* by the Viennese sculptor Karl Bitter.

Justinian (Roman law). Finally there is an empty plinth. At one time there was a figure of Mohammed (Islamic law). It was removed, however, in 1954 when Muslim nations asked the State of New York to do so. Islam is an iconoclastic religion, which forbids representations of Mohammed. On the narrow Madison Avenue side of the building we see Moses (Hebraic law), a central group, *Peace*, by Karl Bitter, then Confucius (Chinese law). We think of multiculturalism as a phenomenon of our own time. But as these figures attest, multiculturalism was certainly around in 1900. Each of the standing figures was done by a different prominent American sculptor. Also on the Madison Avenue facade note the caryatids, *The Four Seasons*, by Thomas Shields Clarke. The themes of the sculpture were developed through consultation with the National Sculpture Society and MAS. During that turn-of-the-century period MAS played a guiding role in embellishing the city with important works of public art.

If at all possible, go inside the courthouse. During normal working hours you can stand in the lobby, which is a designated landmark interior. You see right away that murals play the role on the inside that sculpture plays on the outside. Ask the guard if you can look at the courtroom, through a door on the east side of the lobby. If court is in session, you are allowed, as a citizen, to sit quietly and observe the proceedings. Of course, your eye may also wander about the room, as inevitably it will. (When court is not in session you are allowed into the courtroom at the guard's discretion.) The courtroom was designed under the direction of Gustave Herter of the Herter Brothers, the renowned Gilded Age decorating firm. Murals abound: Behind the bench where the five appellate judges sit are murals by Kenyon Cox, son of Ohio Governor Jacob Cox. Kenyon Cox was a fine painter but an even finer writer and theorist on art; see his brilliant book *What Is Painting?* On the wall opposite are three murals by three different, important artists: Edward Simmons, Edwin Howland Blashfield, and Henry O. Walker. Blashfield, a founder of MAS, was his generation's best American mural painter. Alas, most of his New York works have been destroyed. You have to go to Washington, DC, to see Blashfield's best, the pendentives of St. Matthew's Cathedral. (In New York, one work of Blashfield's with us still is the charming mosaic-adorned stele in Bridgemarket Plaza on the south side of the Queensboro Bridge at 59th Street and First Avenue. The Evangeline Blashfield Memorial, the artist's homage to his wife, who was also prominent in MAS affairs, had been stored away for many years before being restored under the MAS Adopt-a-Mural program.) What will knock your socks off, and much else besides, is the stained-glass skylight dome, a truly magnificent thing, designed by the diplomat-turned-artist D. Maitland Armstrong, who excelled in stained glass and mosaic, two art forms that often go together in the same artist.

**Cross back to the west side of Madison Avenue to view the former north annex of the Metropolitan Life Insurance Company headquarters.**

Across the street from the Appellate Courthouse, occupying the entire block bounded by Madison Avenue, Park Avenue South, and 24th and 25th Streets, is the enormous, squat, jagged, and beautiful former **north annex of the Metropolitan Life Insurance Company**. (**6**) (MetLife has since moved out, and Credit Suisse First Boston is now the primary tenant.) This building has a curious history. In 1929 MetLife announced that it was going to expand its headquarters by building the world's tallest building. Owing, it would seem, to the economic downturn that began just after MetLife's announcement, the building was built in three distinct phases between 1929 and 1950. The architect was Harvey Wiley Corbett, succeeded by D. Everett Waid who closely followed Corbett's design. Each part was seamlessly matched to what came before, in a way that was once a matter of course for architects. The first part, completed in 1932, occupied the full frontage on Park Avenue South, extending west to a point just shy of halfway to Madison Avenue on both 24th and 25th Streets. The part at the southeast corner of Madison and 25th, extending about halfway south to 24th, was finished in 1940; the remainder was completed ten years later. It was in the end built roughly one-third as high as planned. You can well imagine that had it been completed as originally envisioned, it likely would have been the most famous building in New York. We classify it as Art Deco, and indeed it is given the elastic nature of that term. The design is a kind of streamlined eclectic, with classical and romanesque elements and ornamentation in shallow relief (a characteristic of most of what we call Art Deco). On its exterior the building is glacier-like in its Indiana limestone mass.

At each of its four corners is an outsize arched-and-vaulted entryway that often makes people feel they are entering a railroad station or some similarly monumental building. Go in through the entrances at either the northeast corner of Madison and 24th or the northwest corner of Park Avenue South and 24th. The space is coolly majestic like nothing else in New York. You sense that even without air-conditioning you'd feel cool in this lobby—with its luscious crema marble walls and silver-leafed groin vaults—on a 90-degree day. Incidentally, at the northeast corner of Madison and 24th once stood Stanford White's Madison

The Madison Square
skyline, though not
nearly as large as the
downtown or midtown
skylines, nonetheless is
quite extraordinary. The
easy intermixture of tall
and low buildings and
open space has had no
small role in the
neighborhood's late
twentieth-century
renaissance.

The strikingly beautiful
MetLife tower is on the
right. The former
northern annex of
MetLife (center), though
scaled back and never
completed according to
the original plan by
Harvey Corbett Wiley, is
nonetheless one of the
most dramatic Art Deco
buildings in New York.

Square Presbyterian Church, one of his finest buildings, opened shortly after he was killed by Harry Thaw in the roof garden of Madison Square Garden two blocks to the north. Sadly, the church stood for only thirteen years before it was demolished. Such was New York before the Landmarks Law.

**Walk south on Madison Avenue to 24th Street to view the former headquarters of the Metropolitan Life Insurance Company at 1 Madison Avenue.**

MetLife, like New York Life once the nation's largest insurance company, moved its **headquarters** from Broadway and Thomas Street to the northeast corner of Madison Avenue and 23rd Street in 1893. (**7**) The original was a fine building designed by Napoleon Le Brun & Sons. It was replaced by the present modern structure in 1960. As MetLife grew, it expanded to the north, taking up the lot on the southeast corner of Madison and 24th with a 50-story skyscraper completed in 1909 and, until 1913, the world's tallest building. Napoleon Le Brun & Sons patterned it after the Campanile di San Marco in Venice. Around that time, the famous campanile had been knocked down in a storm. MetLife helped raise funds for the campanile's restoration. It seems they felt they could reinforce this act of good will in the public eye by making their new building remind people of the campanile. Forgetting all that, it's a grand building on its own, especially since it was restored (following a modernist mutilation around 1960) in 2000. At night the four-faced clock near the top, as well as the pyramidal top itself, are dramatically illuminated. Napoleon Le Brun, the great Philadelphia architect with credits such as that city's Catholic cathedral and Academy of Music, had nothing to do with the tower; rather, his son Pierre, who moved the firm to New York, was in charge. Under Pierre, the firm did outstanding work in New York, including the Home Life Insurance Building on Broadway just south of Chambers Street and the Church of St. Mary the Virgin on West 46th Street.

**Continue south to 23rd Street and reenter the park along the diagonal pathway.**

In the southeast corner of the park is John Quincy Adams Ward's beautiful bronze statue of **Roscoe Conkling**, dedicated in 1893. (**8**) Conkling, forgotten by most, was a force in Republican politics of the postbellum era.

**Continue along the path heading west toward Broadway. Exit the park at the corner of Broadway and 23rd Street.**

John Quincy Adams Ward, the dean of American realist sculptors, depicted Senator Roscoe Conkling in a bronze statue that, though it attracts little attention, is one of the truly perfect works of sculpture in New York.

Facing out from the edge of the square is the bronze seated figure of **William H. Seward**, by the sculptor Randolph Rogers, dedicated in 1876. (**9**) Seward was a great man who, as secretary of state, was Abraham Lincoln's closest confidant in the cabinet during the Civil War. Seward was also once governor of New York. On the night of April 14, 1865, when John Wilkes Booth shot and killed President Lincoln at Ford's Theatre, Booth's co-conspirator Lewis Powell attempted to assassinate Seward, but failed to do so. A persistent urban legend attaches to this sculpture. Almost every guidebook to New York repeats the falsehood that Rogers, starved for time or funds, placed a head of Seward on a casting of a body of Lincoln the sculptor had done for Philadelphia. I have traced the origin of this story to a letter to the editor of the *New York Times* in 1876. The allegation was made by a writer who identified himself simply as "Artist." Somehow the story gained momentum. People said, rightly, that the body was lean and lanky, which Seward was not. Rogers (the supposed model, by the way, for the character of Kenyon in Nathaniel Hawthorne's greatest novel, *The Marble Faun*, set among the American expatriate artist community in Rome, where Rogers lived

Randolph Rogers's seated figure of Governor William H. Seward is unfortunately plagued by the utterly false story that the sculptor substituted a cast of the body of Lincoln and placed Seward's head on it.

and where he executed the Seward commission) was one of the commercially most successful sculptors of his time and was bound to be resented by envious colleagues. How do I know the story is false? There is only one Lincoln by Rogers in Philadelphia, and one need only compare the two to see that they were not cast from the same original. Nor has anyone ever adduced another Rogers Lincoln to buttress the story. It is simply false.

**Turn north alongside the park and stop near 24th Street at the flagpole to view the Eternal Light Monument.**

This World War I monument, designed by architect Thomas Hastings and sculptor Paul Wayland Bartlett, was dedicated in 1923. (**10**) It has a granite plinth inscribed with the names of significant battles. Surmounting it is an extraordinary bronze flagpole base borne by rams' heads framing great swaths of stylized floral forms. An essential delight of great cities is beautiful flagpole bases, a form of public art like no other in allowing the artist the free elaboration of classical forms.

**Continue north to the intersection of Broadway and Fifth Avenue and cross to the island bounded by Broadway, Fifth Avenue, and 25th Street.**

One of the best places from which to view the Flatiron Building is this triangular island to its north. Where Broadway, cutting its diagonal swath against the gridiron, crosses the avenues, it creates, in the resultant X-pattern, two triangular plots. For example, where Broadway crosses Sixth Avenue, there is the triangular plot of Greeley Square to the south of the triangular plot of Herald Square. (Yes, I know, they are triangles, not "squares.") The triangles here, which do not read so readily as at some Broadway intersections, are the plot occupied by the Flatiron and the plot, called Worth Square, pointing at it from the north. The "square" is so-called for the **Worth Monument**. (11) This granite obelisk, erected in 1856, not only memorializes General William Jenkins Worth, a Mexican War hero, but also marks his burial place. The monument, like the Farragut Monument, was restored under the MAS Adopt-a-Monument program.

Flagpole bases, such as the one on the west side of Madison Square, designed by Thomas Hastings and Paul Wayland Bartlett, offer architects and artists a rare opportunity for sheer aesthetic indulgence.

The Flatiron
Building is no
less a dynamic
presence today
than when it
was built in 1902.
Then it was
viewed by artists
and writers as
the ultimate
symbol of
modernity and
of New York's
restless growth.

Viewed from the side, the Flatiron Building takes on a different character, that of floating planes or screens rippled with Renaissance-inspired terra-cotta ornamentation.

The ornamentation, in terra-cotta, of the Flatiron Building shows how classical devices could be used to convey a quality that was thoroughly up-to-date.

The **Flatiron Building**, one of the city's most fabled buildings, stands at the intersection of New York's two most fabled thoroughfares, Fifth Avenue and Broadway, at 23rd Street. (12) Officially it was the Fuller Building when it opened in 1902, headquarters of the George A. Fuller Company, the large construction firm that had recently migrated eastward from Chicago and brought with it its Chicago architects, D. H. Burnham & Co., said at the time to be the largest architectural office in the world. The Burnham firm's architect in charge was Frederick P. Dinkelberg, an École des Beaux-Arts–trained architect who was prominent in Chicago, where one of his buildings, the Conway Building, is virtually a foursquare version of the triangular-plan Flatiron. The Flatiron was never the tallest building in New York, and it is remarkably less than half as high as the MetLife Tower. But never was a New York skyscraper built freestanding on its own island of pavement, much less at one of the city's most prominent intersections. The sheer visibility of the building, and its triangular form, pointing northward as though to symbolize the relentless uptown progress of the city, made it, in the early 1900s, the very symbol of modernity. (Today we love it because it is old-fashioned.) It attracted artists: Stieglitz and Steichen photographed it; Childe Hassam painted it; H. G. Wells, Ford Madox Ford, and O. Henry described it. But is it any good as architecture? I think it is. The repetitive terra-cotta ornamentation in low relief com-

The cherub is one of the principal formal devices of Western art. No one—before or since—executed them better than the Alsatian Philip Martiny, New York's greatest architectural sculptor.

bines with the shallow oriels to create facades that gently undulate as your perspective shifts when you walk near the building. The walls may seem to be free-floating planes that seconds later resolve into a three-dimensional whole only to break apart again then resolve again. The architectural historian Carl W. Condit once likened the effect to Cubist painting. I think it is more like Impressionism, where the emphasis on the evident brushstroke creates, depending on the viewer's distance or angle in viewing the picture, a kind of dialectic between the flatness of the picture plane and full illusionistic two-point perspective.

It is fascinating to see that this modernism was rendered entirely within the formal vocabulary of Beaux-Arts classicism. Note the "tripartite" composition—distinct base, shaft, capital—pioneered in New York by Bruce Price (American Surety Building) and in Chicago by Louis Sullivan.

**Circumambulating Madison Square is itself enough tour for most people. But let's just take a quick peek at Fifth Avenue in the low 20s. Continue, using the crosswalks, to the west side of the intersection. Turn south on Fifth Avenue and stop midway between 22nd and 21st Streets.**

At the southeast corner of 22nd Street, at 159 Fifth Avenue, is the 1850s **Glenham Hotel**, a handsome Italianate building by Griffith Thomas, once the most prolific architect in New York. (13) To its south at 155 Fifth Avenue is a building that is now the **Rapaport House of United Synagogues of America**. (14) Built in 1893, this beauty was designed by Ernest Flagg as the headquarters and bookstore of Charles Scribner's Sons, one of the fabled publishers of New York. Of special note on its facade, just above the entrance, are two cherubs, one of a small handful of the principal motifs that distinguish classic art of the Western world as distinct from that of other civilizations. The appearance of cherubs alone marks a building as belonging to the long tradition of Greco-Roman art and architecture, the more so when, as here, they are so exquisitely rendered by Philip Martiny, in this writer's opinion the finest architectural sculptor ever to work in New York.

Our tour began with the classical composition of the Donatello-like Farragut Monument and ends with the most moving cherubs in New York. Along the way we have experienced a surfeit of what sets New York among the great classical cities of the world, peer to Vienna or Dublin.

Leaving

**By Subway:** N, R, W at 23rd Street
**By Bus:** M2, M3, M5, M6, M7

## Suggested Reading

*The Art Commission and the Municipal Art Society Guide to Manhattan's Outdoor Sculpture*, by Margot Gayle and Michele Cohen. Prentice Hall Press, 1988. An excellent handbook to Manhattan's outdoor artworks, including those in Madison Square.

*Madison Square: The Park and Its Celebrated Landmarks*, by Miriam Berman. Gibbs Smith Publishers, 2001. A beautifully illustrated book about Madison Square past and present.

*Stanford White's New York*, by David Garrard Lowe. Doubleday, 1992. A very entertaining and perceptive account of the architect whose name shall forever be associated with Madison Square.

*Touring the Flatiron: Walks in Four Historic Neighborhoods*, by Joyce Mendelsohn. New York Landmarks Conservancy, 1998. A very good historical guide to the greater environs of Madison Square.

# 5. Midtown Deco

## MATTHEW A. POSTAL

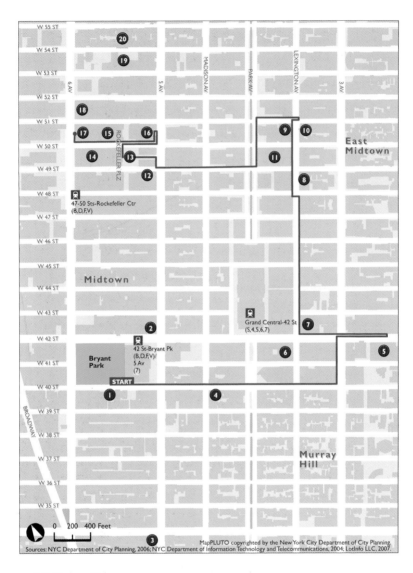

Sources: NYC Department of City Planning, 2006; NYC Department of Information Technology and Telecommunications, 2004; LotInfo LLC, 2007.

## Midtown Deco

**By Subway:** 1, 2, 3, N, R, Q, W, 7, A, C, E to Times
Square–42nd Street; B, D, F, V to 42nd St–Bryant Park
**By Bus:** M1, M2, M3, M4, M5, M6, M7

**Our midtown walk begins on the south side of Bryant Park,
across from 40 West 40th Street, midway between Fifth and
Sixth Avenues.**

For many New Yorkers, Art Deco is the definitive skyscraper style. Fashionable only briefly, from the mid-1920s until the early years of the Great Depression, it drew inspiration from a wide range of stylistic sources, from classical to medieval architecture, as well as French decorative arts, Italian Futurism, German Expressionism, and even Frank Lloyd Wright. The term Art Deco, however, was not coined until the late 1960s. It makes reference to the 1925 Exposition Internationale des Arts Décoratifs et Industriels Modernes in Paris that helped popularize the style, especially among American tastemakers.

The former **American Radiator Building** at 40 West 40th Street was completed just before the exposition, in 1924. (1) Designed by Raymond Hood, one of the most important American architects of the period, the building is of a style that can be most accurately described as stripped neo-Gothic. It has charming figurative corbels along its base, chamfered corners, and abstract ornament that recall Hood's winning design, with John Mead Howells, for the Chicago Tribune Tower in 1922. Isolated from its neighbors on both sides to preserve light and air as it nears the top, the tower diminishes in bulk to form an elaborate crown. Most unusual is the dramatic use of color, principally black and gold. This palette, in contrast to the light-colored, neo-Gothic Woolworth Building, anticipates the sleek, sensuous interiors that make the Art Deco style so popular. Nonetheless, the choice of color was somewhat self-serving. Many observers have compared it to a lump of burning coal, an allusion that would have connected Hood's design to the radiators that the company sold. Greatly admired and floodlit at night, not

Trimmed with gold, the black brick American Radiator Building was
Raymond Hood's first important commission in New York City.

only was the Radiator Building painted by Georgia O'Keeffe but its owners had Hood create a similar design for their London office in 1929. In time, however, the slender proportions hurt their bottom line. With smaller-than-average floors, especially once the space devoted to elevator shafts and hallways was subtracted, the building remained vacant for years. It became the Bryant Park Hotel in 2000, with interiors by British architect David Chipperfield. His first commission in the United States, the public spaces are luxuriously minimal, a handsome counterpoint to the striking exterior.

**Walk east to Fifth Avenue and 40th Street. Stand on the northeast corner to compare two skyscrapers by Shreve, Lamb & Harmon, one of the era's most significant firms: 500 Fifth Avenue, on the northwest corner of Fifth Avenue and 42nd Street, and the Empire State Building, at Fifth Avenue and 34th Street.**

Under the 1916 zoning code, skyscrapers were required to fit into an imaginary envelope, determined by lot size and other factors. Though no height limit was set, setbacks were strongly encouraged, creating a skyline of slender towers, covering no more than twenty-five percent of the site. The genius of the plan was

The building at 500 Fifth Avenue was designed by Shreve, Lamb & Harmon, architects of the nearby Empire State Building.

A textbook example of a setback skyscraper, 275 Madison Avenue was constructed following the stock market crash of 1929.

that it did not stipulate how this should be accomplished, allowing for a great variety of shapes and profiles. Shreve, Lamb & Harmon designed **500 Fifth Avenue**, at the northwest corner of Fifth Avenue and 42nd Street, (**2**) and the **Empire State Building**, on Fifth Avenue between 33rd and 34th Streets, (**3**) in a single year, 1930. Both were built as speculative office towers without a major tenant, and both were executed in a similar streamlined aesthetic. Whereas the 102-story Empire State, the world's tallest building until 1970, is balanced and symmetrical, 500 Fifth rises irregularly, with shallow setbacks that fall away to reveal a slender 60-story tower.

**Continue east on 40th Street and pause at the northwest corner of Madison Avenue to view 275 Madison Avenue on the southeast corner.**

In a city with so many fine skyscrapers, **275 Madison Avenue** may seem ordinary. (**4**) A textbook example of a setback tower, it was designed by architect Kenneth Franzheim for a Houston-based development firm and began construc-

This striking, striped Art Deco skyscraper was designed to house the offices and printing presses of the *Daily News*.

tion in early 1930, several months after the stock market crash of the previous fall. Faced in white brick and black granite, it is a restrained but elegant piece of design, with limited ornament and cascading setbacks. Despite considerable attention from the press, this speculative project was ill-timed, and within a year foreclosure proceedings were brought against the owner.

**Walk three blocks east to Third Avenue and turn north to 42nd Street. Cross to the northeast corner and proceed a half block east to view the former Daily News Building.**

When Raymond Hood designed 220 East 42nd Street in 1928, the *Daily News* was the city's most popular paper. Faced mainly in white brick, the **Daily News Building** suggests a vertical factory, in which the starkness of the walls is relieved only by colored brick spandrels below the windows. (**5**) Though the Museum of Modern Art's architecture curator Philip Johnson frequently criticized the Art Deco style, he admired Hood's evolution as a designer, praising the tower's "spectacular verticalism" as an important step toward a more functional and modern style. The printing annex, directly east, was designed by Harrison & Abramovitz in 1958. Long and relatively low, it is a praiseworthy addition, one that complements but does not copy the tower. The domed lobby is worth a visit, displaying weather instruments and a huge rotating representation of planet Earth. Like the newspaper that commissioned it, this popular feature brings the world down to human scale.

### Return west along 42nd Street to the northeast corner of Lexington Avenue to view the Chanin Building, 122 East 42nd Street, on the southwest corner.

Many of the best buildings of the 1920s, or of any period for that matter, were commissioned by private individuals. The completion of Grand Central Terminal in 1913 attracted increased development to Midtown, especially to the east, along Lexington Avenue, where the Chanin Building and the Chrysler Building stand. The earlier of the two is the **Chanin Building**, 122 East 42nd Street, constructed in 1927–29. (**6**) Irwin S. Chanin began his career in Brooklyn, erecting middle-class homes, and by 1930 he had built a half-dozen theaters in Times Square as well as the twin-towered Century Apartments at 25 Central Park West. Trained as an architect but unlicensed to practice, Chanin worked closely with the architect of record, Sloan & Robertson. Together, they produced a slab-like 56-story tower crowned by a series of buttresses that were originally backlit after dark. As with many buildings from the period, such features are difficult to view from the street and are best appreciated from afar. The lower floors are decorated with two remarkable bands of relief by René Chambellan and Jacques Delamarre, one in terra-cotta and the other in brass. While the lower band illustrates fish and birds, the upper relief is a tour de force of Art Deco graphics, with deep patterns that suggest floral gift wrap. Don't fail to visit the lobby where Cubo-Futurist radiator grilles enliven the small foyers, illustrating a theme that must have been close to Chanin's entrepreneurial heart: the City of Opportunity.

### The Chrysler Building stands on the northeast corner of Lexington Avenue and 42nd Street.

Both inside and out, the **Chrysler Building** epitomizes the Art Deco style. (**7**) Located at 405 Lexington Avenue, this slender 77-story tower gleams, terminating in what architect William Van Alen described as a stainless steel "vertex." Though Van Alen was trained in Paris at the École des Beaux-Arts, little of his earlier work prepares us for this singular building. Consequently, the owner, auto-

The base of the Chanin Building is richly embellished
with distinctive terra-cotta and brass reliefs.

When the Chrysler Building's stainless steel spire was lifted into place on May 28, 1930, it briefly became the world's tallest structure.

mobile manufacturer Walter P. Chrysler, must share some of the credit. As originally planned for William H. Reynolds, the builder of Dreamland Amusement Park in Coney Island, it was envisioned with a Byzantine spire, topped by a glass dome. Hints of this abandoned scheme can be discerned in the rosettes that decorate the lower floors and on the stonework of the mostly hidden east facade, just above the base. Chrysler wanted a building that celebrated his personal success, advertised cars, and attracted tenants. To accomplish this, Van Alen made generous use of industrial materials to create playful, automobile-related motifs that suggest hubcaps and hood ornaments. To add drama, the ultimate height of the project was kept secret. Assembled in the stairwell, the 185-foot-tall spire was riveted into place at the last possible moment, making it, however briefly, the tallest structure in the world—surpassing both the Bank of Manhattan Company Building at 40 Wall Street, which had gained the title only a few months earlier, and the

The incomparable Chrysler Building seen from the south.

Eiffel Tower. Though denounced by some critics as little more than advertising, the Chrysler Building won us over and remains among the city's most loved works of architecture.

To reach the lobby of the Chrysler Building, walk north on Lexington Avenue to the middle of the block, and pass through the deep black archway.

From floor to ceiling, in the side stairwells and the elevators, the lobby dazzles, reminding us that modern design began with the Arts and Crafts movement a half-century earlier and more or less climaxes here. A product of the Jazz Age, the lobby uses materials that are both modern and primitive, juxtaposing smooth metals with exotic woods and marbles, many of which were imported from Africa. Try to catch a glimpse of the elevator cabs: no group from the period is better preserved, and there are four different designs. The Y-shaped ceiling mural conforms to the unusual plan of the lobby and is by the painter Edward Trumbull; it celebrates the production of automobiles and engines as well as the building itself. Many skyscrapers from this period incorporate similar imagery. In a city that was becoming crowded with increasingly tall structures, Trumbull provided visitors with an idealized view of the building, isolated from the surrounding streetscape.

**Exit the lobby. Continue north on Lexington Avenue to 48th Street and cross to the southwest corner to view the former Shelton Hotel, 525 Lexington Avenue, on the east side of the street between 48th and 49th Streets.**

One of the largest groups of hotels built following the First World War is located on or near Lexington Avenue between Grand Central Terminal and 50th Street. Though the earliest ones were built in traditional styles, such as classical and medieval revival, by the end of the decade more adventurous approaches were adopted. Commissioned by James T. Lee, the grandfather of Jacqueline Kennedy Onassis, the former **Shelton Hotel**, at 525 Lexington Avenue, was completed in 1924 and was one of the first buildings shaped by the 1916 zoning code. (**8**) Faced in tan brick and limestone, it was designed by Arthur Loomis Harmon, who later joined Shreve & Lamb and worked on the Empire State Building. The style is vaguely Byzantine, suggesting how the Chrysler Building might have looked in its original scheme. What ornament there is, griffins and blind arcades, enliven and enhance the well-balanced setbacks. Planned as a bachelor hotel, when completed it was one of the tallest in the city, attracting Alfred Stieglitz and Georgia O'Keeffe as residents. For ten years the couple lived in a small, two-room apartment on the 28th floor, producing memorable cityscapes from their perch in the sky.

St. Bartholomew's Church and the neighboring General Electric Building seen from the west.

**Continue north and pause at the northeast corner of 51st Street to view the General Electric Building, 570 Lexington Avenue, on the southwest corner.**

Cross & Cross, a firm whose career began during the Beaux-Arts era and ended with early modernism, was responsible for this impressive tower as well as for the City Bank–Farmers Trust Company Building at 20 Exchange Place and Tiffany's main store at Fifth Avenue and 57th Street. Commissioned by the Radio Corporation of America (RCA) in 1928, the building was never occupied by the company, and **General Electric** became the chief tenant when it was completed in 1931. (**9**) Though the primary material is salmon-colored brick, the details are quite intricate, executed in marble, granite, and terra-cotta. Most of the decoration celebrates the building's original tenant, from a pair of disembodied arms grasping electric bolts to the mysterious figures entwined in the lacy crown, representing the goddess electricity. Buildings of this type aren't typically good neighbors, but this one is. Not only does it continue to delight us but, as viewed from Park Avenue, it forms a surprisingly complementary backdrop to Bertram Goodhue's St. Bartholomew's Church, completed in 1919.

**Look south across 51st Street to 569 Lexington Avenue, the former Summit Hotel, now the Doubletree Metropolitan Hotel.**

This striking structure was designed by Morris Lapidus, one of the most important hotel designers of the past century. He grew up in Brooklyn and began his career in the office of Warren & Wetmore, but he never forgot his Art Deco roots. Like the glamorous stores and sumptuous interiors he created for various retailers during the 1930s, his hotels are full of color, unusual shapes, and ornament. Completed in 1960, the **Summit** was his first and most troubled project in New York City. (**10**) Notable for its curving shape, foam-green elevations, and illuminated stainless steel sign, it fuses together various Midcentury Modern trends, ignoring the more buttoned-up aesthetic that was transforming corporate Park Avenue, one block west. The critical reaction was mixed: though some writers admired Lapidus's attempt to challenge current fashion, others mocked his design, quipping that the new hotel was out of place in Manhattan and "too far from the beach." The owners took these comments seriously, and his lavish and inventive interiors were quickly and completely redesigned.

The Summit Hotel is one of Morris Lapidus's finest surviving works in New York City.

Stylized copper-clad pyramids top the towers of the Waldorf=Astoria Hotel.

**Walk west to Park Avenue and turn south to enter the Waldorf=Astoria Hotel from the Park Avenue entrance. The Waldorf=Astoria Hotel fills an entire block, bounded by Park and Lexington Avenues, 49th and 50th Streets.**

In New York City, the best-preserved hotels of the early twentieth century are the Plaza (now a hotel and apartment building), near the corner of Fifth Avenue and 59th Street, and the **Waldorf=Astoria**. (11) Though the suites and party rooms of the Waldorf have certainly been redecorated, most of the public spaces look as they did when the hotel opened in late 1931. Overall, the style is

Art Deco, but it leans toward classicism. The circulation is grand and symmetrical, with a double-height reception area located deep within the main floor, midway between the avenues. Reached by gently terraced stairs, escalators, and elevators, it is one of the hotel's most elegant rooms, dramatically lit and embellished with gilt plaster reliefs, rich wood paneling, and a remarkable clock—one of the only features saved from the hotel's previous location at Fifth Avenue and 34th Street. Crafted in London for the 1893 World's Columbian Exposition in Chicago, the clock displays portraits of American presidents, sports imagery, and a small reproduction of the Statue of Liberty. Be sure to explore the rest of the main floor, from the floor mosaic and murals in the west foyer to the large elevators that take guests to the grand ballroom, where each year musicians are inducted into the Rock and Roll Hall of Fame and Museum.

**Continue south to 49th Street and turn west to the northwest corner of Fifth Avenue to view the Goelet Building, 608 Fifth Avenue, at the southwest corner.**

Just eight stories tall, the **Goelet Building** is one of the most ornate office buildings in Manhattan. (12) Faced in a thick grid of dark green and white marble, it suggests a jewel box and stands directly south of Rockefeller Center. Completed in 1932, its architects were Victor Hafner and Edward Hall Faile. The retail base, designed to be enclosed with great sheets of plate glass, is surprisingly open and transparent. While some might see it as a precursor to glassy surfaces of the International Style, storefronts such as this may also have laid the groundwork for the recent and often criticized enlargement of many display windows along this fabled shopping street, including several in Rockefeller Center. Step inside the foyer and view the elegant, twisting lobby. Decorated with marble and metal, the elevator doors and cabs are mostly original, as is the marvelous terrazzo floor.

**Turn north on Fifth Avenue. Midway through the block, turn west and enter the Rockefeller Center Promenade, separating 610 and 620 Fifth Avenue.**

Begun during the Great Depression, Rockefeller Center provides a satisfying conclusion to our tour of architecture between the two world wars. When plans to build a new home for the Metropolitan Opera were abandoned in 1930, John D. Rockefeller Jr. decided to change course and pursue a multiblock commercial scheme between 48th and 51st Streets, combining low- and high-rise office structures, stores, and theaters. It was a shrewd gambit, one that only a Rockefeller

The green and white marble Goelet Building stands directly south of Rockefeller Center.

could afford at the time, but he prevailed, creating one of the finest and most influential ensembles of its kind. Saks opened at 611 Fifth Avenue in 1924, filling the entire block between 49th and 50th Streets. The **Promenade (13)**, Rockefeller Center's main east-west axis, is aligned with the department store's neo-Renaissance facade, directing the eye west toward the tower at 30 Rockefeller Plaza. This long and narrow public space is flanked by a pair of identical low-rise structures: La Maison Française, 610 Fifth Avenue, and the British Empire Building, 620 Fifth Avenue. Because the Promenade separated buildings devoted to French and English businesses, it is commonly called the "Channel Gardens." Among the various shops, only one, the Librairie de France, has been here from the start. Paved in quarry stone, the sloping passage offers seasonal plantings, fountains, and benches—amenities that were hard to come by in earlier decades. At the west end is the sunken plaza, used as a restaurant or, during colder months, as an ice-skating rink. Ringed by fluttering flags, landscaped viewing areas, crosstown streets, and the annual Christmas tree, it suggests a European plaza or, perhaps, a multi-

Views west from Fifth Avenue, through the landscaped promenade known as the "Channel Gardens."

*News*, a heroic tribute to the birth of modern media by sculptor Isamu Noguchi.

level town square. Originally planned as a formal garden, designed to draw customers into a subterranean shopping mall, the lower level links all buildings in the complex and leads to the Sixth Avenue subway, an idea borrowed from the concourses in Grand Central Terminal.

**Face west to view 30 Rockefeller Plaza, at the end of the Promenade.**

**30 Rockefeller Plaza** is the tallest and most monumental structure, reaching a height of 850 feet. (**14**) Completed in 1933, it was designed by Raymond Hood, who headed the team known as the Associated Architects, and was originally called the RCA Building. More lively than the former American Radiator Building, it was one of his last and finest designs, with jagged setbacks that terminate in a pinnacle that incorporates a rooftop observation deck. Fusing aspects of the late Art Deco style and streamlined Modernism, this slab-like tower can be described best as a transitional work. What impresses most visitors, however, is the great number of artworks, part of the "Man the Builder" theme and placed strategically above entrances and in lobbies. Colorful three-dimensional reliefs help distinguish one limestone building from the next, identifying public entrances and providing the center with an upbeat iconography. Despite using industrial materials, such as stainless steel and glass, most of the works have an old-fashioned

The artworks throughout Rockefeller Center were carefully coordinated to promote a positive world view. The entrance to 30 Rockefeller Plaza features *Wisdom*, a limestone and glass relief by sculptor Lee Lawrie.

feel, based on romantic classical imagery. Memorable works include Paul Manship's *Prometheus*, on the west side of the sunken plaza; *News*, a stainless steel bas-relief by the Japanese-American sculptor Isamu Noguchi, above the entrance to what was originally the Associated Press Building at **50 Rockefeller Plaza** (**15**); and Giacomo Manzù's *Italia*, a bronze relief at 626 Fifth Avenue.

**To enter the lobby of 30 Rockefeller Plaza, walk around the sunken plaza and use the doors that face the Promenade, passing under Lee Lawrie's *Wisdom, Light and Sound*.**

The ground-floor lobby of 30 Rockefeller Plaza, more than any room in Rockefeller Center, celebrates American optimism and success. Lee Lawrie's work *Wisdom, Light and Sound* incorporates sculpted glass blocks that allow natural light to seep inside the elegant space, especially during the morning hours. There is a beautiful patterned terrazzo floor, worthy of a 1930s movie set, as well as sleek brass railings and radiator grilles. Above the large information desk extends a large mural, *The Triumph of Man's Accomplishments through Physical and Mental Labor*, by the Spanish painter José Maria Sert. Commissioned to replace a 1933 fresco by the Mexican muralist Diego Rivera that Rockefeller viewed as objectionable because it included an image of Communist leader Vladimir Lenin, and that was destroyed, this mural features brushy images of both Abraham Lincoln and Rockefeller Center. Somewhat overblown, Sert's amber-colored mirage seems a bland substitute for what might have been, and what was re-created by Rivera a year later at the Palacio de Bellas Artes in Mexico City. The adjacent hallways, to the west, contain a complementary sequence of murals, *Man's Relationship to Society*, painted by Sir Frank Brangwyn.

**Exit the lobby and walk a few steps north to 50th Street. Turn east to Fifth Avenue and then continue north to the plaza of the International Building, 630 Fifth Avenue, midway between 50th and 51st Streets.**

Built in 1934–35, the **International Building** is located opposite the entrance to St. Patrick's Cathedral, between 50th and 51st Streets. (**16**) The small plaza features a stark limestone arcade and an impressive bronze statue of *Atlas*, also by Lee Lawrie. In contrast to the interiors of 30 Rockefeller Plaza, this marble lobby soars to a height of four stories, dominated by colossal I-beams that rise without interruption to a shimmering copper-leaf ceiling. The abstract sculptures that climb the walls date to 1978 and were created by Michio Ihara. Between the

Paul Manship's colossal statue of *Atlas*, representing both strength and endurance, stands in the forecourt of the International Building, opposite St. Patrick's Cathedral.

freestanding beams, escalators ascend to the mezzanine level, where a bronze bust of aviator Charles Lindbergh is displayed, or descend to the lower level, where some of the center's last original shop fronts from the 1930s can be viewed. Executed with brass and black glass, they are unusually elegant, and it was disappointing to see similar corridors "modernized" by the owners during the 1990s.

**Retrace the path to 50th Street and continue walking west to the northeast corner of Sixth Avenue, sometimes called the Avenue of the Americas, to view Radio City Music Hall at 1260 Sixth Avenue.**

**Radio City Music Hall** contains one of the most spectacular theaters in New York City. (**17**) Home to the dancers known as the Rockettes, it accommodates more than six thousand ticket holders on five levels. The exteriors are similar to the rest of Rockefeller Center, distinguished only by a corner marquee and three colorful enameled brass rondels depicting *Song, Dance, and Drama* by Hildreth Meière. Conceived for live productions, for much of its history it was used for movies that were preceded by lavish stage shows. Seventy-five years of entertainment, however, took its toll, and in 2000 a reported $70 million was spent to restore the splendid interiors, supervised by architect Hugh Hardy, then of Hardy Holzman Pfeiffer Associates, who for many years has served on the board of MAS. The soaring multistory lobby, the glowing fanlike proscenium arch in the auditorium, and even the men's and women's lounges demand a visit and are well worth the price of admission. Donald Deskey is credited for supervising the interior design, collaborating with textile designer Ruth Reeves and painters Ezra Winter, Stuart Davis, and Yasuo Kuniyoshi. Of particular note is the private apartment Deskey conceived for Samuel "Roxy" Rothafel, the theater's first manager. This elegant, wood-paneled, double-height space displays much of its original furniture and can usually be viewed as part of public tours.

A masterpiece of Art
Deco theater design,
Radio City Music Hall.

Along Radio City's 50th Street facade, colorful metal rondels by Hildreth Meière.

Related and worth visiting are *America Today* (1930), a swirling yet realistic mural by Thomas Hart Benton in the lobby of the AXA Financial Center, **1290 Sixth Avenue**; (**18**) the **Museum of Modern Art**, where the original 1939 building, designed by Philip Goodwin and Edward Durell Stone at 11 West 53rd Street, has been handsomely restored (**19**); and the **Rockefeller Apartments**, 17 West 54th Street, built by Harrison & Fouilhoux during 1935–37. (**20**)

Leaving

**By Subway**: B, D, F, V at 47-50th Street–Rockefeller Center
**By Bus**: M5, M6, M7

## Suggested Reading

*Art Deco 1910–1939*, edited by Charlotte Benton, Tim Benton and Ghislaine Wood. Bulfinch Press, 2003. Published in conjunction with the traveling exhibition organized by the Victoria & Albert Museum, this impressive publication features forty essays that consider the development of the Art Deco style and its impact on architecture and design.

*The Art of Rockefeller Center*, by Christine Roussel. W. W. Norton & Company, 2005. There are many books on Rockefeller Center, and this one, focusing entirely on art, is particularly lavish. Also worth seeking out is *Rockefeller Center*, by Carol Herselle Krinsky. Oxford University Press, 1978.

*Form Follows Finance: Skyscrapers and Skylines in New York and Chicago*, by Carol Willis. Princeton Architectural Press, 1995. This book is important because it reminds readers that zoning codes and economics played a critical role in shaping the design of early twentieth-century skyscrapers. Willis is the founder, director, and curator of the Skyscraper Museum, located at the south end of Battery Park City in New York City.

*Skyscraper Style: Art Deco New York*, by Rosemarie Haag Bletter and Cervin Robinson. Oxford University Press, 1975. Hard to find but still valuable, this book contains a thoughtful essay and handsome images.

# 6. Grand Central City

## FRANCIS MORRONE

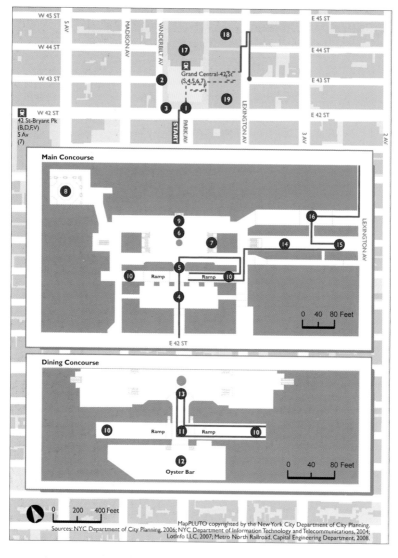

## Grand Central City

1 entrance at 42nd Street and Park Avenue
2 entrance at Vanderbilt Avenue
3 entrance at corner of 42nd Street and Vanderbilt Avenue
4 Vanderbilt Hall
5 bridge
6 Main Concourse

7 east staircase
8 Biltmore Room
9 MetLife escalators
10 ramps to Lower Level
11 Whispering Gallery
12 Oyster Bar & Restaurant
13 Dining Concourse
14 Grand Central Market

15 *Sirshasana*
16 Graybar Passage
17 MetLife Building
18 Grand Central Station of the United States Postal Service
19 former Commodore Hotel

Grand Central Terminal endured years of neglect and "deferred maintenance" that made it a place people avoided. But in the 1990s, a comprehensive renovation of the terminal placed it at the top of New York visitors' must-see lists.

**We will begin our tour at the southwest corner of 42nd Street
and Park Avenue, in front of Ulrich Fanzen & Associates'
Altria Building.**

Look across 42nd Street to the main facade of the terminal. It's a large, monumental building, but what you see is only the tip of the iceberg of Grand Central, which is a vast underground railroad facility. The tracks, platforms, marshaling yards, power plant, and other operations lie beneath all the buildings stretching from 42nd to 50th Streets and Lexington to Madison Avenues.

When the first Grand Central Depot opened on this site in 1871, most of the rail operations took place in open air. Electric trains began to replace steam-powered trains in the 1890s. Just as underground electric trains—the subway—replaced the originally steam-powered elevated railways, beginning with the first IRT line in 1904, so did electricity bring changes to large-scale intercity rail operations like those supported by Grand Central. The idea of enclosed marshaling yards made no sense so long as steam locomotives emitted great clouds of smoke, which needed to dissipate in open air. With electrification, the smoke disappeared.

The New York Central and the New York, New Haven & Hartford Railroads, which jointly operated Grand Central, undertook, beginning in 1903, a massive

The "main" facade of Grand Central Terminal features three huge arches surmounted by Jules-Félix Coutan's *The Glory of Commerce*.

project to convert the terminal's rail operations to electrical power. In doing so, the railroads depressed the tracks and yards below grade—in fact created, for the first time in history, a bi-level railroad facility—then decked them over, creating a whole new neighborhood ripe for the development of office buildings, apartment houses, hotels, private clubhouses, and other buildings—in effect, inventing Midtown Manhattan.

The building you see across 42nd Street opened on February 2, 1913. Two features stand out. First is the "terrace" that forms a base for the building and serves the automobile traffic of Park Avenue. The terminal, to make optimal use of its right-of-way, stands directly bestride Park Avenue. The avenue's traffic rises up onto a viaduct that begins with the vehicular tunnels that pass through the base of the former New York Central Building at 46th Street (now the Helmsley Building), then passes around the east and west sides of 200 Park Avenue (the former Pan Am Building) to form Grand Central's "terrace," funneling onto the viaduct (completed in 1919) that bridges 42nd Street just to your right. Other architects who submitted competition entries for Grand Central's design suggested a vehicular tunnel—like that of the former New York Central Building—

The Park Avenue Viaduct, at 42nd Street, carries the avenue's traffic up to and down from the elevated roadway that then returns to grade at 45th Street.

through the terminal. The viaduct plan, however, by pushing the traffic outside, freed the station interior of such a space-hogging function and made possible the majestic Main Concourse, which we'll see soon.

Stony Creek granite, from Connecticut, faces the terrace, while Indiana limestone faces the upper facade. New York architects began to design stone facades in large numbers in the 1840s. The architects used local stones—the brown sandstones of New Jersey, New York, and Connecticut; marbles from Westchester County; and so on. Toward the end of the century, New York architects fell in love with the limestone of Indiana. On bright clear days, or during the heure bleue of late afternoon, New York's Roman skies (we are, remember, at the same latitude as the Eternal City) interact with the limestone to create subtle kaleidoscopes of shimmering color, as the sun picks out the glittery quartz embedded in the rock. Limestone made New York shimmer like no other city.

The other exterior feature that stands out is the tremendous sculptural group—*The Glory of Commerce*—that crowns the 42nd Street facade. Carved of solid Indiana limestone, the sculpture weighs 1,500 tons. (It's true.) Mercury stands in the middle, with his caduceus and wingèd cap, Roman god of commerce and

Henry Hope Reed calls *The Glory of Commerce* America's greatest work of monumental sculpture.

travel. To his right we see Hercules, embodiment of strength and prowess. To his left, Minerva, goddess of wisdom, peers pensively down upon 42nd Street: In the Roman myths, she serves as the guardian of cities.

Roman, not Greek, gods adorn Grand Central, the classical forms of which derive from the Romans, not the Greeks, via France—and the École des Beaux-Arts. The sculptor of *The Glory of Commerce* was Jules-Félix Coutan. When architect Whitney Warren recruited the Frenchman to the Grand Central job in 1907, Coutan ranked among the foremost sculptors in the world. Coutan's works abound in Paris—we see them at the Hôtel de Ville, the Bibliothèque Nationale, the Palais de Justice, and the Opéra Comique. He served as design director of the Sèvres porcelain works and taught at the École des Beaux-Arts. His only other public work in the Western Hemisphere stands in Buenos Aires, the monument to Carlos Pellegrini. Coutan fashioned in his Paris studio a maquette of the Grand Central group that he shipped to New York, where Donnelly and Ricci, carvers extraordinaire (in New York's golden age of stone carving) working in Long Island City, Queens, made the final full-size sculpture, hoisted in pieces atop the terminal in June 1914. (The stained-glass clockface also comes from Queens—from the Tiffany Studios in Corona.) From start to finish *The Glory of Commerce* took seven years; the whole rest of Grand Central took ten.

It's almost time to go inside. Before doing so note the numerous entries into the building. The **main entrance** faces Park Avenue. (**1**) It's only "main" in relation to the formal composition of the facade. In fact the architects designed the terminal so that several entrances lead directly, ineluctably, to the Main Concourse. For optimal aesthetic impact, it hardly matters which entrance you choose. It's a marvel of such well-thought-out Beaux-Arts buildings that they not only "pull" you toward your destination, in the most natural manner, but also always give your eye a place to come to rest. No matter where you point your eyes, they fall upon a beautiful, sensibly composed surface or termination of an intelligently designed vista.

While each entrance equals any of the others, each also offers something unique. Enter via **Vanderbilt Avenue** (**2**), for example, on the west, and you pass from the street onto a balcony that looks down upon the floor of the Main Concourse. This view from on high excites in a way equal to, though different from, the entrance at 42nd Street and Park Avenue. There you step from the sidewalk into a vestibule that slopes down gently northward to another set of doors, then leads you through the Waiting Room to a beautiful bridge over a pair of sloping walkways connecting the upper and lower levels, then to another slope until, at

The base or terrace of Grand Central Terminal serves as an elevated roadway, wrapping around the station building while carrying the traffic of Park Avenue.

last, you reach the Concourse floor, coming in, as it were, not from "on high" but from "down below," the space rising up as though from your very shoulders. Enter from the corner of **42nd and Vanderbilt** (3), and you traverse a long, downward-sloping ramp that carries you in a great, roller-coaster–like swoosh to the Concourse via its southwestern corner, so that your first view is not longitudinal (as from Vanderbilt Avenue and the balcony), nor latitudinal (as from 42nd Street and Park Avenue), but diagonal, in a northeastern direction. It's worth trying out all three.

**Enter at 42nd Street and Park Avenue under the viaduct and continue straight into Vanderbilt Hall.**

This is the only entrance that takes you through the old Waiting Room, now called **Vanderbilt Hall**. (4) Once benches filled this room. Now it's rented out for functions, exhibitions, seasonal marketplaces, promotional events, and so on. Seldom is it blocked to public passage, however. A bronze plaque on the north wall, just to your left before you reach the bridge to the Main Concourse, hon-

The sloping ramps, designed to facilitate the flow of foot traffic in the terminal, provide the walker with one of the most dramatic architectural experiences in New York.

ors Jacqueline Kennedy Onassis, who as a member of MAS worked to inform and inspire New Yorkers in the 1970s when the then owners of the terminal, Penn Central Corporation, sought via the courts to overturn the city's landmark designation of the building. Lawyers often speak of "landmark cases." This landmark case about landmarks went all the way to the Supreme Court in Washington, where in 1978 the justices upheld the constitutionality of the city's Landmarks Preservation Law of 1965.

When Penn Central soon after went bankrupt, the terminal's new owners, an insurance company from Cincinnati, leased the facility on a long-term basis to the Metro-North Railroad, a commuter line serving destinations north and northeast of the city in New York and Connecticut. Metro-North operates three lines: the Hudson, the Harlem, and the New Haven. The first two follow the old New York Central rights-of-way, formed of Commodore Vanderbilt's nineteenth-century merger of the city's two oldest railroads: the New York & Harlem and the Hudson River Railroads. The New Haven line follows the right-of-way of the old New York, New Haven & Hartford Railroads (which Vanderbilt did not own). Mrs. Onassis, MAS, and Metro-North set in motion the vast reclamation effort that by the late 1990s had redeemed the decaying edifice and made it into one of the most eagerly visited attractions of New York.

## Continue straight. Exiting Vanderbilt Hall, pause on the bridge.

The 1990s renovation brought down walls that blocked the view from the **bridge** (5) of the ramps connecting the upper and lower levels. These sight lines dazzle: The floors plunge downward to a landing directly beneath the bridge, while the golden chandeliers (of which this bridge affords the finest view) remain at a constant level, so that the person on the bridge feels suspended over a falls.

This is also a good spot for an intimate appraisal of the interior's surface materials. The upper walls and the great piers that define the space of the Main Concourse appear to be vast stone supports. In fact, a steel frame supports the terminal. Cast stone curtain walls over the steel columns form the massive piers. "Cast stone" is artificial stone; here, a thin layer of gypsum plaster coats a thin layer of cement. The plaster has been molded and tinted to simulate Caen limestone from Normandy. Through the years, paint and dirt disfigured these delicately tinted beige surfaces. During the renovation, their porous texture made them extremely difficult to clean. Sponge baths failed; pressurized cleaning often makes things worse on porous surfaces. In the end, workers applied a layer of liquid latex to the walls, allowed it to dry, then peeled it away, as in a facial treatment.

The lovely design over the doorways to the lower level tracks features acorns and oak leaves, symbols of the Vanderbilt family. The motto "Great oaks from little acorns grow" referred to Cornelius Vanderbilt's rise from rags to riches.

It worked, and the "stone" is back to something close to the original color.

The lower walls and, in the Concourse, the ticket booths, bear surfaces of a rich Italian marble called Bottocino. The main floors also are of marble, Tennessee pink. This was popular as a flooring material for its durability and comfort underfoot, as well as its handsomeness. Travertine coats the ramp leading down from 42nd Street as well as some floor borders.

From here look at the elaborate chandeliers. They are of gold-plated iron. Look closely and you will see an ornamental motif that soon you will see everywhere you turn in the terminal: acorns and oak leaves. The Vanderbilt motto, "Great oaks from little acorns grow," refers to the Commodore's rise from a poor farm boy on Staten Island to the nation's richest man by the time of his 1877 death. (Historians estimate that in constant dollars the Commodore might be perhaps 50 percent richer than one of the richest Americans of today, Bill Gates.) The bulbous chandeliers themselves, which to many viewers evoke Fabergé eggs, take the shape of acorns. Hecla Architectural Iron Works of

The chandeliers suspended over the ramps are of gilded iron, and were produced by Hecla Architectural Iron Works of Williamsburg, Brooklyn, one of many contributions by the "outer boroughs" to Grand Central Terminal.

Williamsburg, Brooklyn, fabricated these chandeliers as well as all the other ornamental iron in the terminal. This outstanding firm embellished New York with its beautiful ironwork for half a century before the demand for classical ornamentation dried up, and the company with it. (It's nice to know the contributions of the "outer boroughs" to Grand Central: Queens supplied *The Glory of Commerce*, Brooklyn the ornamental iron. Staten Island, of course, provided the Vanderbilts.) In the 1990s renovation, Historical Arts & Casting, an excellent firm in Utah, restored the chandeliers.

### Continue straight into the Main Concourse.

In most railroad stations, the waiting room, not the concourse, is the really splendid space. While Grand Central's Vanderbilt Hall is plenty splendid, it serves merely as an antechamber to the **Main Concourse**, which is like no other railroad concourse in the world. (**6**) A concourse is the part of the station from whence extend the platforms, a place typically more utilitarian in its design than the waiting room.

The architects of Grand Central turned the usual arrangement on its head. In so doing they achieved two things. First, the Concourse functions as what the urban planners Frank Williams and Rei Okamoto called a "mixing chamber." In a dense city, a mixing chamber gathers and dispenses people, serving as a transportation node for a large-scale centripetal and centrifugal distribution of commuters and pedestrians. Without Grand Central we can scarcely conceive of Midtown's people-moving patterns. The architects also achieved an aesthetic effect: a grand space tailored to the constant animation that no mere waiting room could provide.

We have trouble apportioning credit for Grand Central's design. Two firms worked on it: Reed & Stem, of St. Paul, Minnesota, often worked for the New York Central Railroad and specialized in the planning of railroad facilities. We presume that most of the novel planning ideas embodied by the terminal came from the Minnesotans. Warren & Wetmore, of New York City, sullied its lofty reputation by claiming credit for elements of the design that—so courts determined— rightfully belonged to Reed & Stem. Still, no doubt much of the aesthetic design of the terminal came from this outstanding firm, whose other credits include masterpieces such as the former New York Central Building on 46th Street opposite Park Avenue, and the 927 Fifth Avenue apartment building. The third name with which we must reckon is that of the New York Central's chief engineer, William J. Wilgus, who masterminded the whole electrification and air-rights project and

The sky ceiling of Grand Central, in a beautiful, soothing blue-green, was designed by the famous French painter Paul Helleu.

thus, at the least, set the essential contours of the project for the architects.

Yet where in Grand Central does "planning" end and "aesthetics" begin? Grand Central is not a marvel of efficient planning wrapped in an exquisite package. The disparate elements integrate so well that the building makes us think of the beauty of planning and the functionality of aesthetics.

In the Main Concourse note the following: Look up at the mural-painted vaulted ceiling. It crests at 120 feet. The mural shows a blue-green sky drawn with the mythological characterizations of the constellations. People often remark that the constellations appear in reverse. Apparently the artists based their mural on an old manuscript painting that depicted the stars from God's point of view, which is to say a point outside the celestial sphere. No matter. The salient feature of the painting is its rich blue-green background color. All the colors of the Concourse work together in a muted spectrum: the blue-green of the ceiling, the beige of the plaster walls, the pale cocoa of the Bottocino marble, the muted pink of the marble floor. For the person moving through the room, the colors blend into a single light, soothing mood that, when coupled with the loftiness or airiness of the space, induces fresh spirits and uplifted hearts. Some monumentally scaled spaces mean to induce awe; Grand Central's induces warmth.

We credit the mural's design to a once famous French painter named Paul Helleu. He mostly made portraits, and worked for a time out of a New York studio. John Singer Sargent's lovely portrait of M. and Mme. Helleu hangs in the Brooklyn Museum. Helleu made a famous portrait of the beautiful Consuelo Vanderbilt, great-granddaughter of the Commodore. The painter also counted Marcel Proust as a friend and apparently served as a model for the artist Elstir in Proust's À la recherche du temps perdu.

Helleu may have designed the mural; its execution we credit to the Hewlett-Basing Studio. J. Monroe Hewlett—painter, architect, and father-in-law of R. Buckminster Fuller—made from Helleu's designs the cartoons that guided Charles Basing in the creation of the original mural. The Australian-born, École des Beaux-Arts–trained, Brooklyn-based Basing and his assistants executed the original mural in true fresco. Unfortunately, moisture damage so deteriorated the fresco that it was replaced with a new version, of the same design, in 1944. No longer a fresco, the new mural—painted by Basing's onetime assistant, Charles Gulbrandsen—nonetheless replicated all the effects of the original and seemed a suitable solution until the replacement itself appeared to deteriorate. Decades of cigarette smoke cast a thick, sooty film over the mural so that prior to the 1990s renovation the ceiling had acquired

The Main Concourse of Grand Central Terminal is not only a majestic space but, in its brilliant use of materials and colors, a space that makes you feel that all your burdens have been lifted from your shoulders.

a patina of pitch black. The cleaning of the mural ranks among the most dramatic of the several wonderful transformations wrought by the renovation architects Beyer Blinder Belle.

Beyer Blinder Belle added the **east staircase (7)** to the Main Concourse. Apparently a variant design of Whitney Warren's called for stairs at either end of the Concourse. We speculate as to why his eastern one failed to be built. Beyer Blinder Belle and others suggest several possible reasons to which we must add one more: Warren rejected the idea. The presumption that Warren would naturally have sought to "balance" the Concourse strikes me as a fundamental misapprehension of Beaux-Arts principles, which emphasize relational symmetries based on the viewer's shifting perspective, not crude symmetries of plan. The real reason for the new stair had less to do with some putative reclamation of Warren's "original" design than with the need to provide access to a fancy restaurant planned for the east balcony. Overall, I've got to say it works: The restaurant affords a spectacular setting, one that became an instant New York classic.

Doorways leading out to the train platforms line the north wall of the Concourse. The 31 upper-level tracks once served only long-distance trains, like the legendary 20th Century Limited to and from Chicago. Of these tracks, 26 served outbound trains, 5 served inbound. The 5 can handle the capacity of the 26, because while the 26 are stub-end tracks, the 5 inbound tracks loop, describing a sweeping arc along the southern boundary of the underground property beneath 42nd Street, allowing the trains to move continuously from the platforms to the subterranean marshaling yards that stretch from Vanderbilt to Lexington Avenues.

To the northwest of the Main Concourse, directly below the former Biltmore Hotel (which opened, like the terminal, in 1913) at the northwest corner of Vanderbilt Avenue and 43rd Street, the room once called the Arrival Station (now the **Biltmore Room**) received incoming passengers whose egress separated them from the flow of outgoing passengers. (**8**) (If you step out onto one of the platforms off the Arrival Station, and peer behind you onto the tracks, you can clearly see the loop.)

**Proceed to the northern wall of the Main Concourse where the tracks are located, and go left. Keeping the tracks on the right, follow the path to the Biltmore Room on the left.**

Meanwhile, the Lower Level's 17 tracks served suburban passengers. Today, all of Grand Central serves the Metro-North suburban lines; no longer can one take the train from Grand Central to Chicago's Union Station. Amtrak, born of the ashes of the Penn Central bankruptcy, once used Grand Central as well as the West Side's Pennsylvania Station. Ever underfunded, Amtrak chose to consolidate. Penn Station is, well, a *station*, that is, a through stop on the Northeast Corridor line, which, as it happens, is the only profitable route in the Amtrak system. Grand Central, by contrast, is a *terminal*, meaning it is not a through stop but the beginning or end point of any line it serves. While Grand Central is infinitely more beautiful and more efficient than Penn Station, Amtrak had no choice but to consolidate at the other facility.

Banks of **escalators** (**9**) appear in the center of the north Main Concourse wall; these lead to the lobby of the MetLife Building, formerly the Pan Am Building, now also known by its address, 200 Park Avenue.

Built between 1958 and 1963, the Pan Am Building replaced the Grand Central Terminal Office Building, built as an integral part of the terminal complex and containing a beautifully appointed courtyard, to which the Arrival Station provided direct access, for taxicabs. The MetLife Building has the single urbanistic virtue of allowing through pedestrian passage from 42nd to 46th streets via the terminal on the south and the former New York Central Building on the north.

An integral part of the original Grand Central Terminal complex was demolished to make way for the gargantuan Pan Am (now MetLife) Building (1958–63), its exterior designed by the famous Bauhaus architect Walter Gropius.

In the best of Beaux-Arts architecture, all sightlines come to rest naturally on sensibly composed compositions, made possible by both a careful differentiation and an interrelationship of parts.

When built, the Pan Am was the largest office building on earth (measured in square footage of floor area). Its architects, Emery Roth & Sons, delegated the external design to consulting architect Walter Gropius, who borrowed from an unbuilt skyscraper by Le Corbusier from the late 1920s.

**Bear to the right, walking east along the southern wall of the Main Concourse. Exiting the Concourse, turn right. Immediately on the right-hand side is a ramp leading to the Lower Level.**

In some respects, this and its sister **ramp (10)**, on the other side of the bridge, afford Grand Central's finest architectural experience. We see how the planning and the aesthetics blend seamlessly into each other. These ramps connect the Upper Level to the Lower Level—the Main Concourse to the Suburban Concourse. We've already encountered ramps: those leading from 42nd Street opposite Park Avenue to the Main Concourse, and those leading from the corner entrance at 42nd and Vanderbilt to the Main Concourse. Those ramps slope at 10 degrees and 11 degrees, respectively, at their most extreme inclines. (The Main

The Oyster Bar & Restaurant opened in 1913. Its handsome vaulted ceilings are of self-supporting terra-cotta tiles and were built by the company founded by Catalan immigrant engineer Rafael Guastavino.

Concourse floor descends 16 feet below grade when measured from the intersection of 42nd and Vanderbilt.) The ramp you are on now is slightly steeper—12 degrees. Grand Central's designers apparently borrowed the ramp idea from Clinton & Russell's Hudson Terminal of the New York & Hudson Railroad, completed in 1908 on the future site of the World Trade Center. The builders of Grand Central settled on the ramps in 1910 after trying them out on an experimental basis while the terminal continued to function throughout its rebuilding process. From the ramp we can see the bridge from which we viewed the chandeliers. The bridge surmounts a vaulted passage forming one of the visually most pleasing elements of the terminal. Note also how from the ramp the blue-green ceiling of the Main Concourse peeks through above the wall on the north side. This creates a very fine perspective in which the chandeliers overhead feel like nearby stars, and the stars of the sky ceiling, picked out with gilt, recede far into space. Your body's movement downward, the soothing colors, the stars dancing overhead, and the way everything's held in balance by superbly crafted classical devices creates a delirious experience like nothing else in New York architecture.

The *New York Times* waxed rather poetic over the ramps on February 2, 1913:

> As Virgil said of quite a different terminal, "facilis decensus." As Napoleon rode on horseback up to the top of the Campanile, so a mounted policeman from "the finest" might easily ride from Forty-second Street to a train in the lowest level of the terminal without dismounting or causing his horse to stumble. That is what it means to have a station stairless.

Just in case you were wondering.

## Descend to the bottom of the ramp to view the Whispering Gallery and the Oyster Bar & Restaurant.

At the bottom of the ramp we come to the ample landing of that vaulted passage. Its ceiling of terra-cotta tiles—self-supporting in the manner pioneered by the Spanish engineer Rafael Guastavino and constructed by his family's firm—continues to the south through the **Whispering Gallery** into the **Oyster Bar & Restaurant**, the original station restaurant from 1913, directly under Vanderbilt Hall. (**11, 12**) The vaulted landing boasts unusual acoustics, so that those who face inward close to the walls diagonally opposite each other in the landing's corners may converse by a whisper that carries across the vault to the hearer loud and clear. We call this a "whispering gallery," and while its practical uses may seem nonexistent, marriage proposals take place in the space on a regular basis.

In her memoir *Tonight at Noon* (2002), Sue Graham Mingus, the widow of the great jazz bassist and composer Charles Mingus, recalled her early days with him, soon after they met in 1974:

> We walked for a few blocks and caught a cab in front of the Plaza Hotel ....In the middle of our ride, Mingus changed his mind about dinner and said there was something important he needed to show me first. He ordered the driver instead to Grand Central Terminal. When we arrived, he jumped out of the cab and swiftly led me downstairs, hurrying through halls and corridors until we reached a corner that echoed our voices along a wall. I waited at one end of the long wall while he spoke in a low whisper from the other side, unexpected words of tenderness that roared from across the room, shy words of love that slid along the grimy walls of Grand Central as distant and unreal as the graffiti they swept past.

The graffiti of 1974 may be gone. But I still think of Mingus every time I pass through the Whispering Gallery.

One of the outstanding fruits of the Grand Central Terminal renovation of the 1990s was the use of "found space" to create the wonderful Grand Central Market.

**Opposite the Oyster Bar & Restaurant, walk down the short ramp into the Dining Concourse.**

The Suburban Concourse is in length and width the same as the Main Concourse upstairs, though with a much lower ceiling. Post-renovation, the room bears the name "**Dining Concourse**," filled as it is with fast-food eateries and tables and chairs. (13) The Rockwell Group designed the unusual large vinyl chairs.

**Return to the main level via the same ramp. At the top, turn left and continue straight, past the corridor that leads out to Lexington Avenue. Look to the right to enter the Grand Central Market.**

The **Grand Central Market** is a 240-foot-long corridor, the entire length of which is lined with vendors of fresh foodstuffs—meat, fish, coffee, tea, fruits, vegetables, cheese, chocolate, and more. (14) Grand Central Market developed out of the 1990s renovation, a main point of which involved reconfiguring underutilized or disused spaces to increase and improve retailing facilities to make the terminal more profitable. The market operates in "found space." The western half of the corridor had been a storage room; the eastern end, fronting on Lexington, had been a bank. Combined, the two spaces formed a dramatic corridor, bright in design (by Beyer Blinder Belle), fragrant with its foods, and climaxing in the extraordinary modern sculpture *Sirshasana*, by Donald Lipski, just inside the Lexington entrance. (15)

Lipski's sculptural chandelier depicts the spreading branches of an olive tree, hung with 5,000 crystal pendants. The name refers to a yoga headstand that "rejuvenates the body and mind and regulates the flow of energy in the body"—an apt characterization of Grand Central Terminal itself.

**Exit Grand Central Market through doors halfway through the market along the north wall.**

These doors lead to the **Graybar Passage** (16), a corridor shared by Grand Central Terminal and the adjoining Graybar Building.  The skyscraper, completed in 1927, bears more or less stylized Romanesque and Assyrian ornamental details in keeping with the spirit of Art Deco. Sloan & Robertson designed the building for John R. Todd, a developer-manager who soon would be hired by John D. Rockefeller Jr. to build Rockefeller Center, the designers of which worked out of offices in the Graybar Building. The building shows the extraordinary way in which the buildings in the "superblock" bounded by 42nd and 45th Streets and Lexington and Vanderbilt Avenues interlock so as at times to seem a single megastructure.

**Turn right along the Graybar Passage, exiting onto Lexington Avenue. Turn north to 44th Street and cross Lexington Avenue, pausing on the northeast corner for a side view of the (former Pan Am) MetLife Building.**

The **MetLife Building** dominates the north end of the block (17), with an almost unimaginable bulk that wiped out the carefully composed relationship between Grand Central Terminal and the former New York Central Building, causing a generation of New Yorkers to despise the Pan Am. The architectural historian Carl W. Condit famously called it "one of the supreme acts of folly in the history of the city's real estate operations." Younger generations, which grew up with the building, seem more favorably disposed toward it, placing it in the context of a monumental modernism momentarily chic at the beginning of the twenty-first century.

**Walk a little bit north to the middle of the block between 44th and 45th Streets, to view the post office at the southwest corner of Lexington Avenue and 45th Street.**

The Graybar Building on Lexington Avenue is so closely interlinked with Grand Central Terminal that the two buildings share a monumental corridor.

Designed by Warren & Wetmore and built in 1906–9, the **Grand Central Station of the United States Postal Service** predates the terminal itself and ranks as the oldest extant building in the air-rights development area. **(18)** Only half of Warren's stately design was built. He designed the post office, as he did the terminal itself, to support a tall building that might be built at a later date. In 1992 a tower designed by Skidmore, Owings & Merrill rose over the post office. Its deference to the post office and its compatible materials made it the sort of "contextual" addition favored at that time. Today, fashion dictates that such additions differentiate themselves as aggressively as possible from the older structure, as we see with Norman Foster's tower atop Joseph Urban's Hearst Magazine Building on Eighth Avenue at 56th Street. In 1968, when Penn Central proposed a Marcel Breuer–designed tower atop the terminal, the Landmarks Preservation Commission resoundingly said no. One wonders what would happen if the same thing were proposed today.

The Grand Central post office was, like the terminal, designed by Warren
& Wetmore. It was never completed to plan. In the 1980s Skidmore,
Owings & Merrill designed a tower built atop the post office.

Post offices often stood next to railroad stations. Manhattan's General Post Office stood directly to the west of Pennsylvania Station, just as the Grand Central post office stands directly over the terminal's tracks so bags of mail could be dropped directly into railroad cars waiting below.

**Walk south on Lexington Avenue to the northeast corner of 43rd Street to view the former Commodore Hotel, on the southwest corner of the intersection.**

The final building in the "superblock" is the former **Commodore Hotel**. (**19**) Opened in 1919, the Commodore, designed by Warren & Wetmore, once ranked among the largest and most famous hotels in the world. Its shuttering in 1975 symbolized the plight of a bankrupt city spiraling out of control. The city, hoping to revive a moribund 42nd Street, paved the way for the hotel's refurbishment by a young developer named Donald Trump, who hired Gruzen & Partners to glitz up the hotel with some of the sunbelt glamour that pervaded that doleful decade. Presto chango: reflective glass replaced the Commodore's old masonry surfaces, and a gut renovation of the interior yielded the hanging-gardens-of-Babylon lobby with its glass-enclosed "bullet" elevators, à la the Atlanta developer-architect John Portman. The Grand Hyatt New York opened in 1980.

Besides the five buildings of the Grand Central superblock itself, other air-rights buildings include those on Vanderbilt Avenue, which extends from 42nd to 47th Streets, and those along both sides of Park Avenue between 45th and 50th Streets.

The New York Central placed Whitney Warren in overall charge of the greater development. His vision of Park Avenue involved more or less uniform cornice lines stretching south to 46th Street, where the lines would merge with those of the east and west wings of the former New York Central Building, bestride the avenue. These concave wings would then pull the viewer's eye up the shaft of the skyscraper until at its crown a glorious profusion of expertly massed ornamentation culminated in the world's first-ever controlled-aesthetic ensemble of tall buildings. Both in the overall planning vision and in the application of rich classical ornamentation to the railroad's signature office building, Warren demonstrated the infinite adaptability of time-honored forms to new purposes and scales. Indeed, the former New York Central Building deserves to be thought of in the same class of buildings as the Colosseum in Rome.

The last of the air-rights buildings to go up came in 1930: the Waldorf= Astoria Hotel, designed by Leonard Schultze of Schultze & Weaver, arguably our

Warren & Wetmore's New York Central Building (now overshadowed by the MetLife Building) magnificently proved that the time-honored forms of the classical were as suited to the tall, steel-framed office building as to any other building type.

greatest hotel architects. Schultze had worked for many years as Whitney Warren's assistant, and he held the title of "chief of design" on Grand Central Terminal itself. The hotel replaced a generating facility on the east side of Park Avenue between 49th and 50th Streets. A special siding for railroad cars had served the plant, and it remained when the hotel got built. Apparently, no evidence exists to confirm the story that President Franklin Roosevelt or any other U.S. president ever used the siding. That story ranks as one of the two most persistent myths of Grand Central, the other being that colonies of "mole people" have resided in disused tunnels beneath the terminal. The cost and effort of blasting through the schist—so close to grade in this part of Manhattan—to allow Grand Central to go down as far as it did, was an act of prodigious building. The concept that it might have been dug farther and abandoned, or that the space was not used, is a preposterous notion, besides which no evidence of mole people has ever been credibly established.

We end this tour on both celebratory and plaintive notes. The plaintive first: Most of the original air-rights buildings fell to the wreckers' balls after the Second World War, replaced by large and largely characterless office towers of metal and glass. Finally the celebratory: Metro-North, together with many people who worked very hard for a very long time, redeemed Grand Central Terminal itself after decades of "deferred maintenance" had left the building practically a ruin of its original self. Today it shines anew, bearing its creators' classical vision vigorously into a new century.

Leaving

**By Subway:** 4, 5, 6, 7 at Grand Central–42nd Street; B, D, F, V at 42nd St–Bryant Park
**By Bus:** M1, M2, M3, M4, M101, M102, M103, M42


## Suggested Reading

*Grand Central: Gateway to a Million Lives*, by John Belle and Maxine Rhea Leighton. W. W. Norton & Company, 2000. A superbly illustrated book from the outstanding New York City architectural firm that renovated and restored Grand Central Terminal in the 1990s.

*Grand Central*, by David Marshall. McGraw-Hill, 1946. A very conversational book, with some highly offensive period prejudices (such as ethnic stereotypes), but also richly informative.

*The Port of New York*, by Carl W. Condit. University of Chicago Press, 1981. A monumental two-volume work providing not only a detailed (and technical) account of Grand Central Terminal but also a comprehensive description of its role in the vast and intricate rail and terminal system of New York City.

# 7. When It Was New

## Park Avenue

### MATTHEW A. POSTAL

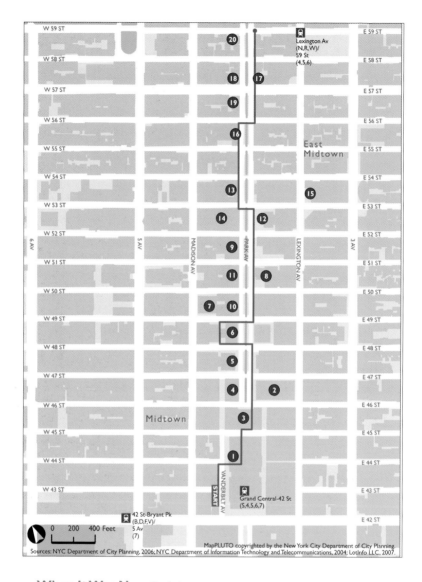

## When It Was New: Park Avenue

1  MetLife Building
2  245 Park Avenue
3  Helmsley Building
4  former Postum Building
5  JPMorgan Chase headquarters
6  Bankers Trust Building
7  45 East 49th Street
8  St. Bartholomew's Church
9  350 Park Avenue
10  300 Park Avenue
11  320 Park Avenue
12  Seagram Building
13  Lever House
14  Park Avenue Plaza
15  Citigroup Center
16  Mercedes-Benz showroom
17  Ritz Tower
18  Davies Building
19  450 Park Avenue
20  500 Park Avenue

**By Subway:** 4, 5, 6, 7 to Grand Central–42nd Street;
B, D, F, V to 42nd St–Bryant Park
**By Bus:** M1, M2, M3, M4, M101, M102, M103, M42

## Begin walk on northwest corner of Vanderbilt Avenue and 43rd Street.

Today, and since the 1950s, the stretch of Park Avenue from 47th to 59th Streets has been Manhattan's most prestigious corporate address. In earlier times, however, it was primarily a manufacturing district, with coal locomotives running at grade, or, later, in an open cut. Following a deadly train accident in 1902, the tracks were electrified and covered below 97th Street, stretching at the widest point almost from Lexington Avenue to Madison Avenue. Apartment houses and hotels soon replaced the factories, and Grand Central Terminal became a major civic gateway. As rail travel declined, however, the New York Central Railroad began to sell these valuable midtown properties. Most of the new owners and tenants were major corporations that wanted offices close to the terminal. In fact, throughout this tour you will be walking on the platform that was built atop the submerged tracks, and perhaps you will feel the gentle vibrations of the trains as they pass below you.

What was created along Park Avenue was strikingly new—shiny glass-and-aluminum-faced towers that signaled the mainstream's embrace of the modern movement. Influenced by European modernism, these so-called International Style buildings stood in sharp contrast to their gradually disappearing neighbors. Whereas most early twentieth-century towers had been faced with masonry—brick or stone—the new use of industrial materials here increased transparency and gave the elevations a sleek, factory-made quality. How these modern buildings related to the street grid was also new. Rather than fill entire sites, setting back

The former New York Central Railroad Building and the MetLife Building, viewed from the north on Park Avenue.

Named for Chauncey Depew, president of the New York Central Railroad, the mostly ignored street on the right runs along the east side of Grand Central Terminal and the MetLife Building. It is mainly used by trucks making deliveries.

in tiers as required by the 1916 zoning code, a few pioneers built slablike towers, rising vertically as three-dimensional objects in space. The Grand Central area is a midtown canyon with buildings of remarkable architectural significance, next to subsequent buildings that met new zoning requirements, but little more.

Towering beside Grand Central Terminal, between approximately 43rd and 45th Streets, rises the 59-story **MetLife Building**, originally known as the Pan Am Building, at 200 Park Avenue. (1) Constructed by developer Erwin S. Wolfson in 1958–63, this flattened octagonal slab was, briefly, the largest office building in the world. Supported by steel stilts, threaded between active railroad tracks, the building was hailed as a major achievement of construction. It has a great many critics, nonetheless, in part because of its enormous size, but also because it interrupts our view of the sky, something that New Yorkers expect when they gaze down the center of Manhattan streets. Faced in light-colored cast concrete, the tower rises from an eight-story rectangular base, with dimensions that recall the Grand Central Terminal Office Building it replaced. Though such celebrated figures as Walter Gropius, founder of the Bauhaus in Germany, and Pietro Belluschi, architect and dean of the School of Architecture and Planning at MIT, consulted on the design, Emery Roth & Sons were the architects of record.

**Walk north on Vanderbilt Avenue to 44th Street. Cross to the east side of the street. Enter the Vanderbilt Avenue lobby of the MetLife Building.**

The lobby is a double-height room with brass-colored escalators and travertine walls. In the early 1960s, air travel was still relatively new. Two major air facilities had recently been completed in the United States, both designed by Eero Saarinen: the TWA terminal at today's John F. Kennedy Airport in Queens, New York, and Dulles Airport, outside Washington, DC. Pan Am, the tower's main tenant, had recently inaugurated transatlantic jet service between New York and Paris, and it wanted an equally memorable headquarters. Among various features commissioned for the public spaces, however, only Richard Lippold's shimmering wire sculpture *Flight*, in the center of the Vanderbilt Avenue lobby, can be viewed. Set on an oval base, it extends to the ceiling where diagonal slits incorporate small bulbs illuminating the wires. A colorful abstract mural by Josef Albers, titled *Manhattan*, was regrettably removed in the late 1990s, and avant-garde Muzak composed by John Cage was never heard by tenants. Because it was planned as an extension to Grand Central Terminal, travelers could arrive at the Pan Am Building by twin-engine helicopter, land on the roof, and make convenient connections to local and suburban trains. Such ideas can be traced to the early twentieth century, when the Italian Futurist architect Antonio Sant'Elia imagined a similar multilevel integration of transit systems. The heliport, however, was used only briefly in the 1960s, and since an accident in 1977 it hasn't been used at all.

**Bear to the left and exit through the building's main lobby onto East 45th Street. Cross the street and take the Park Avenue East passage through 230 Park Avenue. Cross 46th Street to the raised plaza that fronts Shreve, Lamb & Harmon's 245 Park Avenue (1967).**

A rare survivor, the neoclassical former Postum Building, 250 Park, shows how most of Park Avenue looked before the rise of the International Style.

From **245 Park**'s low terrace, we can compare Park Avenue's pre– and post–Second World War character. (**2**) Immediately south, spanning both sides of the avenue, is 230 Park Avenue, the **Helmsley Building**, formerly known as the New York Central Building, a lavish neoclassical (almost Baroque) work by Warren & Wetmore, architects of Grand Central Terminal. (**3**) Directly across the median, to the west, is 250 Park Avenue, originally the **Postum Building**, designed by Cross & Cross in 1925 for the cereal company. (**4**) Both were late additions to the area once called "Terminal City" and conformed to the aesthetic guidelines set earlier by Warren & Wetmore.

Completed in 1929, when the Art Deco style was reaching its height, the Helmsley Building was one of the last important towers built in Manhattan before the Second World War that was inspired by classical sources. At the base, above the entrance, is a clock with sensuous reclining representations of Mercury and Minerva by Edward McCarten. These large statues, like those on 42nd Street, announce the building's purpose and welcome southbound vehicles into the arcades that extend through the base, heading south and onto raised roadways that continue around the terminal to East 40th Street.

**Look northwest to view the JPMorgan Chase headquarters, formerly the Union Carbide Building, at 270 Park Avenue, between 47th and 48th Streets.**

As a street of masterpieces and minor works, Park Avenue is an excellent place from which to judge the ascension of the International Style, especially buildings by the architects Skidmore, Owings & Merrill. Founded in Chicago in 1936, Skidmore, Owings & Merrill first opened a Manhattan office in 1937. Several of the firm's most outstanding works will be viewed en route, including the former Union Carbide Building, now headquarters of **JPMorgan Chase**. (**5**) Occupying an entire block, it was completed in 1962 and consists of a 53-story tower and a 13-story wing facing Madison Avenue. Clad with black matte aluminum panels, the slender decorative stainless steel mullions project and rise without interruption, enhancing the composition's powerful vertical thrust. For this project, Skidmore, Owings & Merrill's chief designer Gordon Bunshaft collaborated with Natalie de Blois, one of the first women to play a significant role in American corporate architecture. For three decades she worked for Skidmore, Owings & Merrill, in the New York City and Chicago offices. At the base of the tower is a shallow plaza; though hardly generous, it enhances the openness of the glazed ground floor, providing a pleasant buffer between the street and the elevators that, like many buildings along this section of Park Avenue, rise from the mezzanine level.

Immediately north of JPMorgan Chase is 280 Park Avenue, built in stages for **Bankers Trust** between 1960 and 1968. (**6**)

Several teams of architects worked on this building, including Emery Roth & Sons; Shreve, Lamb & Harmon; and the prominent industrial designer Henry Dreyfuss. Though many recently constructed banks had glass and aluminum facades,

Erected by the chemical producer Union Carbide in 1962,
270 Park Avenue is now the headquarters of JPMorgan Chase.

The former Bankers Trust Building, 280 Park Avenue, is one of Manhattan's last buildings to conform to the 1916 zoning law.

such as the luminous Manufacturers Trust Company branch by Skidmore, Owings & Merrill at 510 Fifth Avenue, in the early 1960s these materials fell from favor and architects began to make greater use of precast concrete panels, which could be fashioned into various shapes, colors, and textures. Since the exterior is what most people see, it has a great impact on how a building and its tenants are perceived. For his contribution, Dreyfuss designed the front tower's 6-by-12-foot window frames, a series of beveled cast-concrete and quartz projections that highlight the gridded fenestration and increase the play of sunlight and shadow. Though not entirely successful, it was a unique project in Dreyfuss's prolific career, anticipating the limited role star architects and designers may play in highly publicized projects, whether they are Frank Gehry or Philippe Starck.

**Walk north to 48th Street, cross Park Avenue, and walk west along the north side of the street. Midblock, turn right and walk through the raised covered passage.**

Planned with a private driveway for bank executives and important guests on the right (east) side, the passage features a sinewy brass metal screen by sculptor Stephanie Scuris that separates pedestrians from arriving vehicles. Though conceived as an extension to Vanderbilt Avenue, this passage, like the one directly south, attracts relatively few users.

**At the end of the passage, look across 49th Street toward the low structure.**

Oscar Nitzchke designed **45 East 49th Street** for Addo, a Swedish business machines manufacturer, in 1957. (**7**) Born in Germany, this talented architect worked with Wallace Harrison on many high-profile projects during the 1940s and 1950s, such as the United Nations Headquarters and the Alcoa Building in Pittsburgh. Originally used to market German typewriters, English "duplicators," and Swedish computers, during the late 1960s and 1970s 45 East 49th Street was leased to Aeroflot Soviet Airlines and, later, China Air. Though the color scheme was changed to orange to meet the needs of the current tenant, an international bank, the architectural firm Gensler retained the building's original facade, with its eye-catching canopy, as well as the open-plan interior. Sadly, this charming building is threatened and may be replaced by a ventilation facility to serve an expanded Grand Central Terminal.

**Return to the east side of Park Avenue and turn north to 51st Street. Pause on the steps of Bertram Goodhue's St. Bartholomew's Church (8) to view 350 Park Avenue on the northwest corner of the intersection.**

Emery Roth & Sons designed **350 Park Avenue** for the Uris Brothers, a major commercial developer, in 1958. (**9**) Faced in gray glass, this is boilerplate modern, with a facade that ruffles few feathers. Roth immigrated to the United States in the 1890s and designed many memorable apartment buildings, including the San Remo and the Eldorado on the Upper West Side. His sons, Richard and Julian, continued to operate the firm after his death in 1948, focusing mainly on office buildings. Over the next two decades, they worked on approximately seventy structures in Manhattan, making the firm, arguably, the city's most prolific. In later years, they mainly specialized in production work, participating in the construction of both the World Trade Center (with Minoru Yamasaki) and the Citigroup Center (with Hugh Stubbins). (See pages 206, 207.) Roth & Sons designed **300 Park Avenue** and **320 Park Avenue** in a similar manner, but neither retains

This striking commercial structure at 45 East 49th Street was constructed for Addo, a design-conscious manufacturer and distributor of business machines.

the original glass facade. (10, 11) For instance, 320 Park Avenue was completely redesigned in 1995 by Swanke Hayden Connell Architects, a firm closely associated with Donald Trump. Now faced with slabs of granite and dark glass, the building has splashy metal details and a rooftop mast that recall the decorative flourishes of the late 1920s. More respectful, perhaps, though hardly better, was the complete refacing of 300 Park Avenue in 2000. This office building originally had a cream-colored glass facade, but the new treatment, by Moed de Armas & Shannon, features tinted glass and bland aluminum paneling.

**Continue north and stand in the plaza of the Seagram Building, 375 Park Avenue, between 52nd and 53rd Streets. (12)**

To the northwest, between 53rd and 54th Streets at 390 Park Avenue, stands **Lever House**, the building that began Park Avenue's aesthetic transformation and changed the trajectory of twentieth-century architecture in New York City. (**13**) Designed by Gordon Bunshaft of Skidmore, Owings & Merrill in 1950–52, Lever House was innovative on several different levels. When the British soap and detergent manufacturer decided to erect a North American headquarters here, it was a mainly residential street. Not only were the materials that were chosen new—only the United Nations Secretariat Building had a similar curtain wall of greenish blue glass—but the juxtaposition of two slablike masses—a single story raised on aluminum-clad pillars above a spacious public plaza, and a slender vertical tower—pronounced that a new architectural era had begun. Modestly scaled and perfectly

Emery Roth & Sons produced many office buildings with crisp, tinted glass curtain walls in the 1950s, including 350 Park Avenue.

Lever House, viewed from the southeast.

The neo-Renaissance Racquet & Tennis Club opened when most buildings along this section of Park Avenue were residential.

balanced, Lever House was designated a landmark in 1982. It was one of the first buildings constructed after the Second World War to receive such recognition, and MAS played an important role in the process, calling on such celebrities as Jacqueline Kennedy Onassis, Brendan Gill, and Philip Johnson to help gain political support. Despite wide acclaim, by the 1990s the distinctive curtain wall had seriously deteriorated. The building's architects had limited experience with glass skins, and when panels later failed they were replaced with pieces of a slightly different shade, giving the facades a checkerboard-like quality. In addition, leaks began to compromise the steel structure, requiring the current owner, RFR Realty, to replace the entire skin. Skidmore, Owings & Merrill supervised the splendid $25 million restoration, and today it is difficult to distinguish any changes. Be sure to explore the open courtyard, with gray and white marble benches by American sculptor Isamu Noguchi, as well as a raised planting bed (conceived as a platform for contemporary sculpture) that extends through the glass wall and into the lobby. This memorably minimalist volume is comparable to Philip Johnson's Glass House, which was, coincidentally, completed a year before construction of Lever House began. The lobby is used for exhibitions and generally open to the public; enter through the revolving doors to observe the artworks and the strangely silent urban ballet that surrounds you.

*The Virgin Mother*, a bronze sculpture by Damien Hirst, was a temporary installation in the courtyard of Lever House.

The Seagram Building, the only work by Mies van der Rohe in New York City, is one of his best.

Directly south, behind the Racquet & Tennis Club (McKim, Mead & White, 1917) is **Park Avenue Plaza**. (**14**) Extending through the block, from 52nd Street to 53rd Street, this 44-story green glass tower was designed by Skidmore, Owings & Merrill and completed in 1981. The partner in charge of the project was Raul de Armas, later of Moed de Armas & Shannon. Taking cues from its celebrated neighbors, Park Avenue Plaza (55 East 52 Street) has green glass elevations like Lever House, and the green and white marble walls of the atrium are similar to the benches that flank the pools of the Seagram Building. These public interiors are pleasant and attractive, with seating and restrooms.

### Descend the stairs of the plaza and face east.

The Seagram Building, built in 1954–58, is probably Park Avenue's best-known structure. Discussed in guidebooks, college textbooks, and numerous architectural publications, it is considered a key work by the German-born architect Ludwig Mies van der Rohe and one of the finest examples of the International Style. For some, however, the Seagram is difficult to love. Austere and precisely composed, it may require repeat visits and, like the product the liquor company sells, it improves with age. Mies always hoped to design a glass skyscraper; he proposed several for Berlin in the early 1920s, but most of what he built prior to the 1950s was low and horizontal, such as the Farnsworth House in Plano, Illinois, and the campus of the Illinois Institute of Technology in Chicago. Initially, Charles Luckman, an architect and a former executive at Lever Brothers, of the firm Pereira & Luckman, was hired. He proposed a marble-faced tower with a prominent Seagram logo over each entrance, a bulky and uninspired design that the owner's daughter, architect Phyllis Lambert, strongly opposed. She persuaded her father, Samuel Bronfman, to visit the nearby Museum of Modern Art (MoMA), where they consulted with Arthur Drexler, the museum's architecture curator. Three master architects were suggested: Frank Lloyd Wright, Le Corbusier, and Mies. In the end, Mies, who made Chicago his home, was selected. He collaborated with Philip Johnson, who had organized an important survey of the architect's work at MoMA in 1947, as well as with the firm Kahn & Jacobs, who served as associate architects. The 38-story

A deep plaza provides an elegant forecourt to the lobby of the Seagram Building.

tower that resulted is an icon of mid-twentieth-century modernism, but many of the most distinctive features were actually drawn from the antique tradition, such as the low podium on which it sits, the freestanding pillars that recall a classical colonnade, and the facade itself, which is clad with a bronze veneer, a brownish metal closely associated with classical Greek sculpture. (Incidentally, to retard oxidation, each year the surface must be washed and rubbed with lemon oil.) Mies was a modernist, but he had enormous respect for his predecessors, and this crisply designed masterpiece succeeds in bridging two, often disparate, styles.

The serene glazed lobby is visible from the street and plaza. No signs or shops, not even a newsstand, detract from the dramatically lit travertine walls that enclose the elevator shafts. Restaurants, however, were always part of the scheme. The interior of the Four Seasons, at 99 East 52nd Street, adjoining the tower to the rear, was left to Johnson and includes the memorable and airy Grill and Pool Rooms; the Brasserie at 100 East 53rd Street has been playfully redesigned in a modernist vein by Diller & Scofidio (2000). Be sure to take a peek at these handsome but contrasting spaces; the owners generally welcome visitors, particularly at off-hours.

**Walk north to the south corner of 53rd Street to view the Citigroup Center, located on Lexington Avenue, between 53rd and 54th Streets.**

One block east of Lever House and the Seagram Building is the **Citigroup Center**, designed by the Boston architect Hugh Stubbins. (**15**) Constructed in 1972–78, it is one of the most Corbusian buildings in New York City, employing many of the devices promoted in the Swiss-French architect's 1923 manifesto, *Toward an Architecture*. It is an impressive late modern work. The 59-story aluminum-clad tower rises from a massive central core and four colossal pilotis, and the windows are arranged in continuous ribbons. The angled roof was originally conceived for tiered private gardens. Though neither greenery nor solar panels would be installed on the roof, it had a striking shape that, perhaps inadvertently, helped reignite interest in the city's skyline and the pursuit of eye-catching pinnacles.

**Cross to the west side of Park Avenue and continue north. Pause near the corner of 56th Street to view the Mercedes-Benz showroom at 430 Park Avenue.**

Clad with aluminum panels, the Citigroup Center rises nine hundred feet.

Frank Lloyd Wright often visited New York City during his last and most prolific decade, staying in a three-room suite at the Plaza Hotel that some writers have called "Taliesin East." Construction of the Solomon Guggenheim Museum (1943–59) dominated much of the aging architect's time, but he also built in upstate New York and New Jersey, as well as the modest **Mercedes-Benz showroom**. (**16**) Commissioned by Maximilian Hoffman and originally planned to display Jaguars, it occupies the north half of the ground floor of a 1920s office building that was refaced in the 1950s and again in 2000. Though the automobile models have changed and much of the furniture is from a later date, the curving ramp and turntable are original (and the turntable is still operable). The showroom is one of only three projects that Wright completed in New York City. As with the museum, the spiraling form of the showroom takes inspiration from marine animals and recalls Wright's 1949 plan for the V. C. Morris Gift Shop, now an art gallery, in San Francisco.

**Return to the east side of Park Avenue and continue north to the southeast corner of 57th Street.**

Where Park Avenue meets 57th Street are three buildings associated with Emery Roth, each from a different decade and displaying a distinctive style. The earliest, at the northeast corner, is the **Ritz Tower**, at 465 Park Avenue. (**17**) Originally a residential hotel, it was designed by the firm's founder in 1925–27, in association with Thomas Hastings, formerly of Carrère & Hastings, architects of the New York Public Library on Fifth Avenue. Hastings probably consulted on the design and produced the tower's fine neoclassical details. Home to journalist Arthur Brisbane, William Randolph Hearst, and the celebrated French restaurant Le Pavillon, the 540-foot-tall Ritz Tower was the tallest residential building in New York City when it was completed.

On the northwest corner is 460 Park Avenue, also called the **Davies Building**. (**18**) Owned by Hearst's widow, the infamous silent-film star Marion Davies, it was completed in 1954 and was Manhattan's second structure to be faced entirely in aluminum, following Emery Roth & Son's National Distillers Building at 99 Park Avenue. Fabricated in two-story sections, the faceted, gray curtain wall was, reportedly, erected in just fourteen hours.

The last of these three Roth projects is **450 Park Avenue**, built between 1968 and 1972. (**19**) Located on the southwest corner, this understated 33-story slab parallels the avenue and adjoins a narrow plaza to the west. The graceful building has a podlike, space-age quality, with soft-edged window bays grouped in threes. The facade is exceptionally smooth, incorporating flush tinted glass and black aluminum panels that recall Skidmore, Owings & Merrill's Marine Midland Bank Building at 140 Broadway (1967) in lower Manhattan and 919 Third Avenue (1971) at 55th Street. Though Emery Roth & Sons set few stylistic trends and never attained the exalted status of some contemporaries, this large and amazingly prolific office produced good quality work and helped define what corporate modernism was in mid-twentieth-century Manhattan.

**Continue north to the northeast corner of 59th Street to view 500 Park Avenue on the southwest corner.**

Critic Ada Louise Huxtable aptly described **500 Park Avenue** as "a kind of Pazzi Chapel of corporate design." (**20**) Built by Skidmore, Owings & Merrill in 1958–60 for Pepsi-Cola (now headquartered in Westchester, but originally based in Manhattan), this ten-story corner building rises in isolation, set off from neighbors by a thin slot of black granite that allows the projecting glass volume to float above a shallow raised plaza. When the building opened it had a public gallery in the base, and actress Joan Crawford on its board of directors. (Her fourth husband,

A 1970s design by Emery Roth & Sons, 450 Park Avenue.

Alfred Steele, had been the company's chairman and chief executive officer.) In later years, it was owned by the Olivetti Corporation, the high-style Italian office machines company. Natalie de Blois, working again under Bunshaft, was responsible for the building's elegant and almost weightless-looking design. As in much of the firm's best work, the seams that divide the horizontal plate glass, aluminum panels, and paving are carefully aligned, creating a distinct sense of control and precision. These qualities, however, were gradually lost over time, overshadowed by highly visible choices made by clumsy interior designers, as well as insensitive maintenance. In 1986, a 39-story apartment tower, designed in a complementary fashion by James Stewart Polshek & Partners, was built behind 500 Park Avenue on 59th Street. The two buildings were joined and a major restoration was begun. At that time, the facade's transparency was recognized as important, and rules were

The former Pepsi-Cola Building is one of the finest International Style buildings in New York.

introduced to determine what types of window treatments and ceiling fixtures would be allowed. Less than three decades old, the Pepsi-Cola Building was one of the earliest twentieth-century modern structures to be restored in Manhattan. The changes had a significant effect on the building's exterior, as well as on subsequent restoration projects elsewhere, setting the stage for an ongoing reevaluation of the modern movement and its contribution to the city's built environment.

Several blocks north, between Park and Lexington Avenues, is a stimulating group of mid-twentieth-century houses that may also be considered: 101 East 63rd Street, designed by Paul Rudolph in 1967, the Edward Durell Stone house of 1956, at 130 East 64th Street, and the white brick Edward A. and Dorothy Norman house, 124 East 70th Street, built by William Lescaze in 1940.

Leaving

**By Subway:** 4, 5, 6, N, R, W at Lexington Avenue / 59th Street
**By Bus:** M101, M102, M103

## Suggested Reading

*Four Walking Tours of Modern Architecture in New York City*, by Ada Louise Huxtable. Museum of Modern Art and the Municipal Art Society of New York, 1961. Concise and well written, this slim and out-of-print guide was commissioned soon after MAS inaugurated its walking tour program in 1956. Huxtable, who would become the first architecture critic at the *New York Times*, was a former staff member in the Department of Architecture and Design at MoMA.

*The International Style*, by Philip Johnson and Henry-Russell Hitchcock. W. W. Norton & Company, 1997. Johnson founded the Department of Architecture at MoMA in 1932. This illustrated book, published independently in 1932, attempted to define modern architectural principles and aesthetics. Though the department's first catalogue, "Modern Architecture: International Exhibition," quickly went out of print, *The International Style*, in various editions, has always remained available and popular.

*The Pan Am Building and the Shattering of the Modernist Dream*, by Meridith L. Clausen. MIT Press, 2004. Love it or hate it, this gargantuan office tower is an important example of midcentury modernism and deserves greater attention.

*Skidmore, Owings & Merrill: SOM Since 1936*, by Nicholas Adams. Phaidon, 2007. Despite great prominence, relatively few books have examined this prolific American firm. Adams focuses on a select group of international projects, including Lever House and the Pepsi-Cola Building.

*Toward an Architecture*, by Le Corbusier. Getty Research Institute, 2007. A lively and passionate manifesto for modern architecture, this 1923 publication remains a key architectural treatise. Originally translated as *Towards a New Architecture*, this edition, with an essay by architectural historian Jean-Louis Cohen, is said to be closer to the author's original intent.

# 8. Midtown Since Modernism

## East 57th Street to Columbus Circle

MATTHEW A. POSTAL

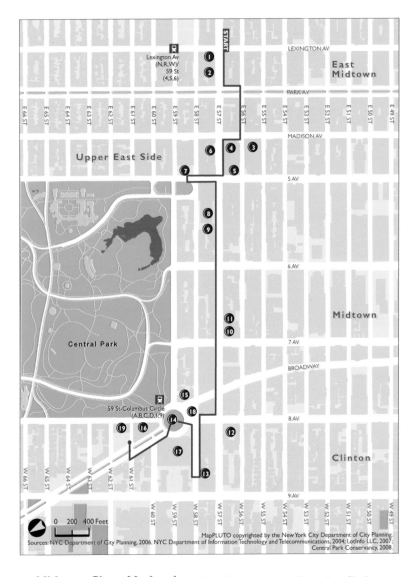

## Midtown Since Modernism: East 57th Street to Columbus Circle

1   135 East 57th Street
2   115 East 57th Street
3   former American Telephone
    & Telegraph (AT&T) Building
4   former IBM Building
5   Trump Tower
6   19 East 57th Street

7   Apple Store
8   9 West 57th Street
9   29 West 57th Street
10  Carnegie Hall
11  Carnegie Hall Tower
12  Hearst Tower
13  Hudson Hotel

14  Columbus Circle
15  240 Central Park South
16  Trump International Hotel
17  Time Warner Center
18  Museum of Arts and Design
19  15 Central Park West

## Begin the tour at the southeast corner of Lexington Avenue and 57th Street, looking northwest.

This walk carries forward the story of architecture in New York City from the time when the city was down and bankrupt to the more prosperous present day. We examine buildings that fall into the loose stylistic categories known as late modern, postmodern, and contemporary. Incentive zoning will be discussed and the ways in which government policy has been used to shape projects, especially by encouraging atriums, those indoor spaces that blur distinctions between public and private space. Though the record for such amenities is, admittedly, mixed, it has had a dramatic effect on midtown's character, resulting in taller structures, some of which include amenities that serve the public well.

Postmodernism arrived in the late 1970s; the architectural community had grown tired of metal and glass, turning toward the playful ideas promoted in Robert Venturi's widely read manifesto *Complexity and Contradiction in Modern Architecture* (published by the Museum of Modern Art in 1965) as well as *Learning from Las Vegas*, which Venturi coauthored with Denise Scott Brown and Steven Izenour. These books criticized modernism's abstract character, urging architects to develop designs that would speak to the public through the manipulation of applied decoration. In most cases, they looked to the past for inspiration, reviving the use of ornament and materials found in nature. Typical of the postmodern movement was **135 East 57th Street**, designed by Kohn Pedersen & Fox in 1987. (1) Commonly called KPF, the firm attracted many corporate clients, and this midtown tower is one of their more distinctive works. Thirty-four stories tall, it has

At Lexington Avenue
and 57th Street, a
marble tempietto in a
rare corner plaza.

a concave facade that pulls away from the busy intersection to create a rare corner plaza where a marble tempietto, circled by low benches, stands. Like many
structures built during the 1980s, the references are to classical antiquity—particularly imperial Rome—but as viewed through an Art Deco lens that gives the
gray granite facade a somewhat cartoonish quality. Nevertheless, it is an interesting design, better than most, and a good place to start examining what became
of modernism in the late twentieth century.

**Walk west to midblock, stopping opposite 115 East 57th Street.**

The Galleria at **115 East 57th Street** was one of Manhattan's first mixed-
use buildings. (**2**) Designed by David Kenneth Specter (with Philip Birnbaum) in
1973–75, it consists of a thin apartment tower that rises from an eight-story base
containing stores, offices, and a public atrium. Part of a broader planning strategy
to invigorate commercial districts by permitting increased residential use, such
schemes, it was hoped, would transform midtown into a 24/7 community. Faced

The Galleria, incorporating apartments, offices, and a public atrium,
was designed by David Kenneth Specter in the mid-1970s.

with brick, granite, and exposed steel, the lower floors have a severe, almost Brutalist quality. The residential entrance faces 57th Street, as do the stairs that descend to a dark atrium that turns and connects with 58th Street. An interesting yet flawed model, this multilevel interior suffers because it is located below grade, causing few people to use it because it lacks natural light and because most of the surfaces are faced with dark materials. Though recent changes have improved the situation somewhat and attracted new tenants, the now strangely colorful atrium has lost some of its historic charm. At the top of the building is a multistory glass penthouse, visible from a distance, that was planned for, but never occupied by, Stewart R. Mott, an heir to the General Motors fortune. Mott considered himself an urban farmer and hoped to use the 7,500 square feet of rooftop terraces to cultivate vegetables.

**Continue west to Park Avenue. Turn south to 56th Street and then west. Pause near the northeast corner of Madison Avenue to view 550 Madison, the former AT&T Building, between 55th and 56th Streets.**

For most people, 550 Madison Avenue defined the style known as Postmodernism. Faced with acres of pink speckled granite, the tower terminates in a highly visible broken pediment. Constructed by the **American Telephone & Telegraph Company** in 1977–83 and now owned by Sony USA, it was designed by Philip Johnson during the period he was associated with John Burgee. (**3**) Johnson's design was big news; not only was the building commissioned by a major corporation but it signaled the architect's most public rejection of the International Style and the movement he had helped create four decades earlier. Johnson had worked alongside former Bauhaus director Mies van der Rohe on the Seagram Building during the mid-1950s, and some quipped that his use of pink granite and classical detailing made the tower seem like the earlier building "in drag." Johnson's classicism was both criticized and celebrated in the press; it was *the* moment in his career and he cherished the spotlight, appearing on the cover of *Time* with an image of the tower and the headline "U.S. Architects: Doing Their Own Thing."

The former AT&T Building is a collage of elements borrowed from the Italian Renaissance and later periods. While the general form suggests a colossal grandfather clock like those produced by Thomas Chippendale in the late eighteenth century, the arcade was inspired somewhat by the Galleria Vittorio Emanuele (1861) in Milan, and the base, as originally built with low rectangular arcades flanking a recessed round arch, Brunelleschi's Pazzi chapel (1429–61) in

Completed in 1983, 550 Madison Avenue (the former AT&T Building) made Philip Johnson a celebrity and helped popularize postmodernism.

Florence. Planned when AT&T was still the nation's largest employer, by the time the building was completed, antitrust suits had broken up the company into significantly smaller firms, christened "Baby Bells," making the freshly completed headquarters an unnecessary luxury. The building was purchased by Sony in 1992, and the firm of Gwathmey & Siegel oversaw major changes to the public spaces, converting the ill-used front plazas beneath the tower into profitable retail space and enclosing the rear arcade. Approved by the Department of Planning, these changes made the arcade into an enclosed atrium but ultimately detracted from Johnson's original vision. Look closely at the handsomely executed details and peek into the vaulted lobby, the side arcades, and the atrium that connects 55th and 56th Streets.

Leafy bamboo trees, plentiful seating, and abundant natural light make the atrium at the former IBM Building, 590 Madison Avenue, one of Manhattan's finest.

The 57th Street facade of the former IBM building with its dramatic cantilevered corner entrance on Madison Avenue.

**Cross Madison Avenue, passing *Levitated Mass*, a fountain by sculptor Michael Heizer, and enter the atrium of 590 Madison Avenue on the northwest corner.**

The former AT&T Building, the former **IBM Building (4)**, and **Trump Tower (5)** were constructed simultaneously with public spaces that allowed the owners to produce structures of increased height and bulk. Though the AT&T Building received the most attention, the now-enclosed rear arcade feels constricted and has become overly commercial, with conspicuous advertising for Sony products. Trump Tower at 721 Fifth Avenue (Der Scutt and Swanke Hayden Connell, 1983) contains a vertical shopping mall that, though spatially interesting, suffers from an overdose of polished brass and Italian marble. Of the three examples, the atrium of the former IBM Building is arguably the most successful. Designed by the architect Edward Larrabee Barnes, the sunlit glass-and-steel pavilion takes up approximately half the lot and is planted with clusters of leafy bamboo trees. This is exactly what the Department of Planning had in mind when incentive zoning was proposed, and it remains, despite a new owner and minor changes, one of Manhattan's most heavily used atriums. The bulky tower, however, is heavy and dull, faced with polished gray-green granite and ribbon windows. The most noteworthy feature could be the corner entrance, set on a diagonal at Madison Avenue and 57th Street. Lacking any visible means of support, this anxiety-provoking feat of engineering caused a future patron, Park West Realty, to insist that Barnes redesign the entrance to 535 Madison Avenue (which was then under construction) by inserting a nonbearing column, whose purpose was purely psychological.

**Proceed on a diagonal path through the atrium to the revolving door on the north wall. Exit onto 57th Street and stand opposite 19 East 57th Street, the LVMH Building.**

By the mid-1990s, architects began to turn away from postmodernism, seeking inspiration, once again, in the aesthetics of the mid-twentieth century. Among the first buildings in Manhattan to reflect this trend was **19 East 57th Street**, built for LVMH, the French luxury goods conglomerate. (**6**) Not surprisingly, they chose a Frenchman, Christian de Portzamparc, and this was the architect's first work in the United States. Clad with white and light green glass, this sleek, faceted tower gently twists as it ascends, terminating in a transparent volume that serves as a party space. Like many of his French colleagues, Portzamparc likes to experiment with glass, juxtaposing opaque, translucent, and fritted panels. Artfully inserted between a pair of masonry towers, one from the 1920s and the other from 1996, the tower's sculpted form serves as a stylishly modern counterpoint to its more traditional neighbors.

**Walk west to the corner of Fifth Avenue. Turn north, stopping midblock between 58th and 59th Streets outside the Apple Store.**

This popular branch of the **Apple Store** opened to great fanfare in 2007. (**7**) Designed by Dan Shannon of Moed de Armas & Shannon, the entry pavilion stands in the plaza of the former General Motors Building at 767 Fifth Avenue. Though the design is elegant, part of the excitement was connected to the surrounding plaza's rebirth as a genuine public space. As planned by Edward Durell Stone in 1965–68, the tower originally rose behind a sunken plaza, similar to the

Christian de Portzamparc, winner of the Pritzker Prize in 1994, designed this memorably curvaceous office tower for LVMH.

one in Rockefeller Center. The plaza was an unequivocal commercial and critical failure, as few people descended the stairs to shop or eat, and much of the time the subterranean commercial spaces sat vacant. When the building changed hands in 2005, a new strategy was proposed, requiring approval by the City Planning Commission. In exchange for filling in the sunken plaza, the owner agreed to upgrade the public amenities, adding flexible seating and fountains on either side of the store's entrance. Most striking, however, is the cube's remarkable transparency which, when the light cooperates, makes it almost disappear. Not only are the walls entirely glass (with discreet titanium hardware), but so is the cylindrical elevator and spiral stairs that lead to the sleek retail space below. Simple as it as, this prominent project forecasts a major role for glass in the twenty-first century.

**Face west and look briefly down 58th Street, past Bergdorf Goodman, to the rear sloping facade of 9 West 57th Street. Return to 57th Street and walk west until you see the building's main facade.**

In the 1970s, 57th Street began to change. Long associated with cultural pursuits and high-end retail, older low-rise structures gave way to several gargantuan office towers. The best of the group, **9 West 57th Street**, was designed by Gordon Bunshaft, chief designer at Skidmore, Owings & Merrill. (**8**) Built in 1968–74, it was one of the architect's last works and, arguably, among his finest. Though the International Style was definitely in decline, Bunshaft remained committed to the simple abstract forms that once made it fresh. Fifty stories tall, the tower runs through the block to 58th Street and features a pair of gently sloping brown glass facades that writers have compared to a ski slope or bell-bottomed pants. Though Bunshaft claimed the shape was determined by the zoning code, the contours and exposed bracing recall the Eiffel Tower when viewed from the east or the west. In addition, the sloping profile uncovers **29 West 57th Street**, built for Chickering and Sons, a Boston piano manufacturer. (**9**) (Completed by the architects Cross & Cross in 1924, the crown is decorated with reliefs that advertise the Legion of Honor medal that the piano manufacturer received at the Paris Exposition in 1867.)

At the base of 9 West 57th Street, the travertine trim extends both into the lobby and out onto the sidewalk where a large freestanding number "9" identifies the building's address. Created by the celebrated graphic designer Ivan Chermayeff, this orange Pop art–inspired icon plays splendidly against the dark facade (recalling the earlier placement of Isamu Noguchi's *Red Cube* that stands in front

Despite its marvelous transparency, this popular 24/7 branch of the Apple Store in the plaza of 767 Fifth Avenue is hard to miss.

Completed in 1974, 9 West 57th Street was one
of architect Gordon Bunshaft's final commissions.

of the Marine Midland Building at 140 Broadway). Because the sculpture is installed in the middle of a public sidewalk, owner Sheldon Solow has to pay a monthly rent to the city to keep it there.

**Continue west along the north side of 57th Street to the northwest corner of Seventh Avenue to view Carnegie Hall on the southeast corner of the intersection.**

The simultaneous development of postmodernism and the growth of the preservation movement stimulated a renewed appreciation for architectural history. Not only did new buildings frequently incorporate traditional ornament but architects were often asked to, or decided to, create contextual designs that acknowledged their neighbors, as is the case with **Carnegie Hall** and **Carnegie Hall Tower**. (10, 11)

Despite the high regard that musicians and the general public justifiably hold for Carnegie Hall, this institution has always been a work in process. All but the legendary auditorium has been substantially altered since the building opened in 1891, from the removal of the original mansard roof in order to create artists' studios in 1894 to the creation of a new lobby in the mid-1980s. With the construc-

Both address marker and Pop art sculpture, this steel number "9" was created by the talented graphic designer Ivan Chermayeff.

tion of Carnegie Hall Tower at 152 West 57th Street in 1991, a building of such height that would not generally be considered a good neighbor, architect Cesar Pelli made the best of a difficult situation. Cladding the exceptionally thin slab of the new building with panels of brown, orange, and green brickwork, he complements but does not copy Carnegie Hall and, in effect, fuses the two buildings into a single postmodern composition with Carnegie Hall serving as the launching pad for a much taller tower. (This strategy is similar to the one Pelli adopted at the World Financial Center during the mid-1980s, where his complex of five setback office buildings originally stepped up toward the World Trade Center.)

Carnegie Hall has three handsome performance spaces. In addition to the neoclassical-style main hall credited to Louis Sullivan's partner Dankmar Adler and to Richard Morris Hunt, there is the more intimate Weill Recital Hall on the third floor, and Zankel Hall, located beneath the main stage and entered from 881 Seventh Avenue. Completed in 2003, Zankel's wood-paneled auditorium was designed by Richard M. Olcott, of Polshek Partnership Architects. To the south, on 56th Street, is the domed tower called CitySpire at 150 West 56th Street (Helmut Jahn, 1987), and to the east, just beyond the small structure housing the Russian Tea Room, is Metropolitan Tower, 147 West 57th Street, designed by the architects Schuman, Lichtenstein, Claman & Efron in 1987. Faced entirely with black glass, the sleek and shiny elevations of Metropolitan Tower provide a pleasing counterpoint to Pelli's colorful brick tower.

**Continue west to the northeast corner of Eighth Avenue to view Hearst Tower on the southwest corner of the intersection at 300 West 57th Street.**

**Hearst Tower** is one of Manhattan's most recognizable new buildings. (12) Visible throughout Midtown and especially from Central Park, the tower seems best appreciated from up close, at an angle, and from below. It is from this vantage point that the tower's jagged profile appears most dramatic, offering glimpses into the oddly shaped interiors. Few recent designs, even Frank Gehry's IAC Building in Chelsea, have created as much passion. (See page 89.) Designed by Foster + Partners, the Hearst media headquarters was completed in 2006 and sits atop the hollowed-out core of Joseph Urban's Hearst Magazine Building, built in 1927–28. To realize the project, Hearst first needed the approval of the Landmarks Preservation Commission, which it won easily, in part due to the general quality of the scheme, but also because the yellowish cast-stone structure had originally been planned as a skyscraper. It was a bold decision, resulting in an

Constructed in the late 1980s, the soaring Metropolitan Tower (left) and Carnegie Hall Tower (center) juxtapose distinct and dissimilar approaches to postmodernism.

Hearst Tower, a dramatic essay in glass and stainless steel, is one of New York City's most exciting new skyscrapers.

impressive new work of architecture, but possibly setting a bad precedent for additions to historic structures. Foster's tower, positioned at the center of the base, is a study in contrasts. There is hardly any relationship between old and new; rather than use similar materials, Foster chose dark glass and employed a diagonal grid of trusses, called a diagrid, clad with stainless steel panels. Perhaps inspired by Louis Kahn's unbuilt 1957 design for a skyscraper, or even by a honeycomb, it is a spectacular piece of engineering, equal to many of the firm's finest works. As originally planned, the base was to be a pubic atrium, but due to post 9/11 security concerns the mezzanine level is off-limits and is used as the staff cafeteria. The soaring escalator lobby, however, can generally be visited. It features *Ice Falls*, a gentle waterfall designed by Foster, James Carpenter, and James Garland; *Riverlines*, a mural by Richard Long; and the enormous pillars that hold the tower aloft. Built from almost ninety percent recycled structural steel, Hearst Tower was one of the first buildings in New York City to receive a gold LEED rating from the United States Green Building Council, a significant accomplishment.

**Turn north along Eighth Avenue. Turn west along the south side of 58th Street and stop near Ninth Avenue to enter the Hudson Hotel, 356 West 58th Street.**

While the **Hudson Hotel** was built as a long-term residence for young women in 1928, only the modest alterations to the lower floors hint at the memorable sequence of interiors found within the building. (13) Enter via the glass doors that glide open without a touch and travel up the glowing escalator to a darkly atmospheric reception area. The French architect and designer Philippe Starck designed the 1,000-room hotel and its marvelously decorated spaces, turning the second floor into an eclectic hipster's den with his own furniture designs as well as unusual pieces by Antonio Gaudí, Ingo Maurer, and the Dutch firm Droog Design. Behind the reception area is an outdoor garden, a brick-walled restaurant, and a library. The latter rooms have high ceilings and strong personalities. Whereas the focus of the library is a large pool table, the restaurant has communal wooden tables and feels like a college dining hall or a monks' refectory. Just behind the escalators is the glass-walled Hudson Bar, featuring a backlit floor and a ceiling mural by Francesco Clemente. This last interior serves to remind us that Ian Shrager, the impresario behind the hotel, also created two legendary nightspots, Studio 54 and the Palladium. In a hotel where the wood-paneled guest rooms are notoriously small, as little as 140 square feet, the public interiors become the main attraction.

Shrager helped create the idea of the boutique hotel, and the Hudson Hotel remains one of his finest achievements. Because design matters so much to Shrager, he has worked with some of the world's more daring designers, renovating the Gramercy Park Hotel with painter-filmmaker Julian Schnabel (2006) and creating 40 Bond Street (2007), an apartment building in NoHo, with the Swiss architects Herzog & de Meuron. Take time to explore the Hudson, especially when the weather is warm and the garden is open. And lastly, try not to take these well-designed interiors for granted. As products of fashion, few historic hotels, or restaurants for that matter, survive in New York City. Even the lobby of Schrager and Starck's celebrated Royalton Hotel—just two decades old—reopened in 2007 with a completely new decor.

**Return to Eighth Avenue, turn north, and cross into the center of Columbus Circle.**

Despite endless automobile traffic, the plaza located at the center of **Columbus Circle** is remarkably peaceful. (**14**) Redesigned by the Olin Partnership during 2002–5, the plan was deceptively simple, consisting of low granite walls that are just the right height, sound-canceling fountains, and comfortable wooden benches. Many said it couldn't be done, but the designers have created an extremely appealing space, one that attracts crowds. MAS played a role in the redesign, sponsoring a competition in 1997. Though the proposals were quite speculative (Olin and Machado & Silvetti envisioned a "halo-like structure" set on pylons), the event helped focus much-needed attention on the site's potential and led to the eventual selection of the designers.

Most of the structures that surround Columbus Circle are of recent vintage, dating from the 1990s to the present. The earliest are both civic monuments, the statue of Christopher Columbus (1892) by Gaetano Russo, from which the circle and Columbus Avenue got their names and, at the corner of Central Park, the Maine Memorial (1901–13) by Attilio Piccirilli. On the east side of Broadway is **240 Central Park South** (Mayer & Whittelsey, 1940), an early example of an apartment building shaped by the aesthetics of European modernism. (**15**) Innovative features include corner windows, metal balconies, and a colorful mosaic above the entrance, *The Quiet City*, by the French painter Amédée Ozenfant, the cofounder (with Le Corbusier) of the art movement known as Purism. On the north, between Central Park West and Broadway, is the **Trump International Hotel**. (**16**) Built as the Gulf & Western Building (Thomas E. Stanley, 1969), during the mid-1990s it was converted into

This new plaza, redesigned by the Olin Partnership in 2002–5, is an excellent vantage point from which to view Central Park and the recent buildings that surround Columbus Circle.

Set on axis with Central Park South, the Time Warner Center is the latest and probably largest mixed-use development in Manhattan.

apartments and given a bronze skin marked by angled piers designed by Philip Johnson.

The largest structure is all but impossible to ignore. Completed in 2003, the **Time Warner Center** is a colossal mega-mixed-use development, curving along the west side of Broadway between 58th and 60th Streets. (**17**) Mustafa K. Abadan, a design partner at Skidmore, Owings & Merrill, designed the complex following more than a decade of debate concerning the project's impact on the neighborhood. Many critics, including MAS, opposed an earlier plan by Moshe Safdie, which would have cast much longer shadows across the park for much of the day. Set on axis with Central Park South, the completed scheme brings together a multilevel shopping mall, offices, an apartment building, three music venues operated by Jazz at Lincoln Center (designed by Rafael Viñoly, 2004), and a hotel. The public interiors are designed in an uninspired faux Art Deco style, with granite paneling relieved by occasional metal details. One feature deserves special comment: the cable-net glass wall, located opposite the escalators. A tour de force of transparent low-iron glazing, it was created by James Carpenter, who was also responsible for the *Dichroic Light Field* (1994–95), a shimmering wall relief that can be seen on Columbus Avenue, between 67th and 68th Street, as well as

Glass technologist James Carpenter, a MacArthur Fellowship recipient in 2004, created the nearly invisible window wall that faces Columbus Circle.

the diagonal waterfall, *Ice Falls*, in the lobby of Hearst Tower. This 150-foot-high window acts like a canvas or video wall, providing shoppers with a continuously changing view of Columbus Circle and the park.

**Using the crosswalk, return to the west side of Columbus Circle. If you wish, explore the Time Warner Center, or turn southeast and face 2 Columbus Circle, located between Broadway and Eighth Avenue.**

Few New Yorkers will soon forget the controversy that swirled around this site and the building that the **Museum of Arts and Design** replaced at 2 Columbus Circle in 2008. (**18**) Though modernism and minimalism dominated American high culture in the mid-twentieth century, some architects and collectors expressed doubt in the 1950s, namely Huntington Hartford II, who founded the Gallery of Modern Art here in opposition to the aesthetics promoted by the all-powerful Museum of Modern Art. He found a sympathetic collaborator in the architect Edward Durell Stone, who designed MoMA's original building (with Philip L. Goodwin) in 1939 but in recent years had begun to enrich his work with references to earlier and more varied traditions. Stone was particularly fond of decorative screens and often designed facades lacking windows. The Gallery of Modern Art opened in 1964; though some early exhibitions were well received, the building's quirky design was soundly criticized. Minimalism remained fashionable, and few critics could relate to the sumptuous and somewhat eccentric detailing. Hartford closed his museum in 1969, and though it continued to function, on and off, as a cultural venue, it fell into a sad state of disrepair. In this tarnished condition, it attracted few admirers. Though interest in saving the building gained support in the mid-1990s, time quickly ran out. The Landmarks Preservation Commission unfortunately refused to hold a public hearing on its future, and the city, which became the owner in the 1980s, sold it to the American Craft Museum, now renamed the Museum of Arts and Design. Seeking a fresh identity, the structure has been completely gutted and refaced with a layered glass and terra-cotta facade designed by Portland, Oregon, architect Brad Cloepfil of Allied Works Architecture.

**Walk north on Broadway to 61st Street. Cross to the east side of Broadway to view the rear facade of 15 Central Park West.**

Architect and historian Robert A. M. Stern designed **15 Central Park West**, completed in 2007. (**19**) Consisting of two towers linked by a domed entrance pavilion, it is, in terms of style, one of New York City's most traditional new buildings. Stern's office has done an admirable job of designing a contemporary structure that gently fuses classical, Art Deco, and contemporary modes. He drew inspiration from some of Manhattan's most famous older apartment houses, namely 740 Park Avenue (1929), River House at 435 East 52nd Street (1931), and 19 West 72nd Street (1936). While there is some classical ornament, overall the treatment is quite austere, allowing six thousand tons of limestone to define the building's luxurious character. Filling an entire block, the taller west tower rises from a trapezoidal commercial base that conforms to Broadway, while the east tower fits well into the lower scale of Central Park West. Viewed from the park, the two buildings read as a single structure, stepping up to an asymmetrical crown with a neoclassical loggia. In financial terms, 15 Central Park West has been one of New York City's most successful new apartment buildings. In contrast to buildings recently constructed in Chelsea, or changes to nearby Lincoln Center by the architects Diller Scofidio + Renfro, the developer followed a tastefully cautious strategy, taking limited aesthetic risk but, in the end, producing a dignified piece of design as well as record profits.

Leaving

**By Subway:** 1, A, C, E at 59th Street–Columbus Circle
**By Bus:** M5, M7, M104, M10, M20

## Suggested Reading

*Architecture After Modernism*, by Diane Ghirardo. Thames & Hudson, 1996. A thoughtful discussion of architecture in the late twentieth century, from Robert Venturi and Disney to Jean Nouvel and Tadao Ando.

Curbed.com. Begun in 2004, this popular blog addresses current real estate issues and architecture in New York. Chatty, opinionated, and useful.

*Delirious New York: A Retroactive Manifesto for Manhattan*, by Rem Koolhaas. Monacelli Press, 1997. First published in 1978, this is an important book by an important architect. Written in hard times, when faith in New York and many cities was low, it celebrates the skyscraper and the "culture of congestion."

*Metropolis.* Published monthly, this well-designed magazine (and its Web site at metroplismag.com) addresses contemporary architecture and design, especially in New York City.

*New York: A Guide to Recent Architecture*, by Susanna Sirefman. Konemann, 1997. A concise, pocket-sized guide to the five boroughs, covering the 1980s and most of the 1990s.

*Public Art of New York*, by Jean Parker Phifer, W. W. Norton, 2009. From outdoor sculpture in public plazas and landscapes to murals and works of art in lobbies accessible to the public, organized by neighborhood, with maps suitable for a walking guide, this book focuses on how exemplary works of public art enrich urban public space.

# 9. Country in the City

## Central Park

FRANCIS MORRONE

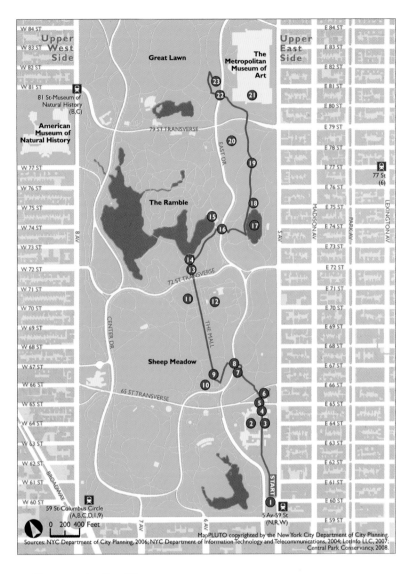

## Country in the City: Central Park

1  Scholars' Gate
2  Central Park Wildlife Center
3  Arsenal
4  Delacorte Music Clock
5  Denesmouth Arch
6  Tisch Children's Zoo
7  Balto
8  Willowdell Arch
9  Robert Burns; Sir Walter Scott; Fitz-Greene Halleck statues
10  *Indian Hunter*
11  *Eagles and Prey*; Beethoven; Schiller; Victor Herbert statues
12  Naumburg Bandshell
13  Bethesda Terrace
14  *Angel of the Waters*
15  Loeb Boathouse
16  Trefoil Arch
17  Conservatory Water
18  Alice in Wonderland
19  Glade Arch
20  Cedar Hill
21  Metropolitan Museum of Art
22  Graywacke Arch
23  Obelisk

**By Subway:** N, R, W to Fifth Avenue / 59tth Street
**By Bus:** M1, M2, M3, M4, M5

Central Park is one of the greatest works of art of the nineteenth century, the summation of the romantic ethos of its era, a saga of America's self-definition, and a defining act of urban reform from a time when New Yorkers, and Americans, struggled to find remedies to social ills so rapidly multiplying in the industrial cauldron of the city that their amelioration appeared to many to be impossible. Perhaps what is most remarkable about Central Park is that we cannot see where the work of art ends and the project of social reform begins.

Make no mistake: The industrial cities of the first half of the nineteenth century were horrible. In New York, the mass immigration of the 1840s and 1850s increased by many times the overall social misery of the city. The overcrowding, the squalor, young industries' need for surplus labor, the abandonment of children, crime and delinquency, wholly inadequate sanitary infrastructure, and contagious diseases threatened to make the city an insupportable environment and lent legitimacy to Thomas Jefferson's view that cities were at best a necessary evil and, at worst, as he had said of New York, "a cloacina of all the depravities of human nature."

But New York had time and again shown its ingenuity. The Commissioners' Plan of 1811 was a farsighted blueprint for the future northward growth of the city—and even staked out an area bounded by 23rd and 34th Streets and Third and Seventh Avenues as the "Grand Parade," which was 1811-speak for "Central Park." The Erie Canal (opened in 1825) was a larger public-works project than any that had ever been undertaken in Europe—and it was accomplished solely by the people of New York. The Croton water system, opened in 1842, may have been late in coming, but when it came it proved to be a model of its kind. New York knew how to do.

The Grand Parade of the 1811 plan never came to be. The land, which in those days of primitive transportation lay within a region of country houses and farms, was soon enough directly in the path of a city ferociously extending northward. From the Grand Parade to Madison Square, the space was whittled down to its present dimensions: 23rd to 26th Streets, Madison to Fifth Avenues. A nice residential square, hardly a metropolitan park. Some New Yorkers thought there was no need for a metropolitan park on Manhattan Island. The island was narrow, "ventilated" by its cradling rivers. Pockets of green existed in the burgeoning residential squares—Madison Square (see page 107), Washington Square, Gramercy Park—and in the pleasure gardens, with names such as Niblo's Garden and Jones' Wood, where one paid a fee for all manner of bucolic entertainment on private grounds that were a feature of nineteenth-century Manhattan. Yet the residential squares were places for the well-to-do, and the pleasure gardens were yielding to development—John Jacob Astor had carved up Vauxhall Gardens into the upper-class Lafayette Place neighborhood. Meanwhile, one of the first acts of the municipal government of the city of Brooklyn had been to establish at the city's outer edge a great cemetery, Green-Wood (hard by the border of the city of Brooklyn and the town of New Utrecht), which, though meant to be the final resting place of the good people of Brooklyn, in fact attracted picnickers, promenaders, and lovers to its manicured lawns and splendid lookouts.

Above all, London had shown the way in attempting to import the countryside into the city as a means of remedying urban ills—and as a means of kick-starting the development of new high-class residential districts. Regent's Park, built by the architect John Nash for his friend the Prince Regent, was conceived as a residential development in which town houses would be so situated amid the extensive grounds as to provide a simulacrum of the countryside where upper-class Englishmen preferred to spend their time. St. John's Wood had taken shape along similar lines—what we call *rus in urbe*, the Latin phrase ("country in the city") referring to a particularly British value. The public parks movement from which Central Park arose began in Britain. The major figure was a nineteenth-century genius named Sir Joseph Paxton. Architecture buffs know him as the creator of the Crystal Palace at the Hyde Park exhibition of 1851. His expertise in greenhouse construction came from his position as chief landscape gardener of the enormous Chatsworth estate of the Duke of Devonshire. Paxton then undertook to create public parks that, though tied in with real estate developments (as in fact were New York's parks), nonetheless sought also to be places of respite and refreshment amid some of the most hellish cities on earth.

Like Liverpool. In 1850 a New York journalist, Frederick Law Olmsted, went abroad to write a book called *Walks and Talks of an American Farmer in England*. After disembarking in Liverpool, Olmsted was profoundly affected by Birkenhead Park, Paxton's creation across the Mersey. It had recently opened in 1847 and "is acknowledged to be the first publicly funded park in Britain," according to its Web site.

Coincidentally, also in 1850 America's leading landscape gardener, Andrew Jackson Downing, paid a visit to London, where he hired a young British architect, Calvert Bowyer Vaux (pronounced "*vawx*") to come work in the Downing firm in Newburgh, New York, just north of the city. Olmsted was already a devotee of Downing; Vaux was already a devotee of Paxton. Yet in 1850 Olmsted and Vaux knew nothing of each other. That would change.

To make a long story short, Downing and the newspaper editor and poet William Cullen Bryant led the public parks movement in New York, calling for a large park that would bring the calming influences of nature within reach of the industrial city's beleaguered and benighted denizens. Olmsted followed them in their call. In 1853 the city acquired most of the land for the future Central Park, from 59th to 106th Streets and from Fifth to Eighth Avenues. It was a perfect rectangle made up of lots extracted from the platted gridiron of Manhattan streets. Olmsted, though a journalist with a known byline, had for a while lacked steady employment, which lessened his desirability to the opposite sex—and he very much wanted to get married and have a family. He finagled his way into the position of superintendent of the clearing of the land for Central Park.

Meanwhile, Downing, the presumptive designer of the park, died tragically in a steamboat accident on the Hudson River. The design job devolved upon a civil engineer named Egbert Viele, who, though a brilliant engineer, presented a design universally acknowledged as dreadful. This led to an open competition for the park's design. Downing's assistant Vaux had a plan. To better his chances in the competition, he knocked one day on Olmsted's door. The two together, by combining Vaux's design genius and Olmsted's practical knowledge of the landscape conditions and political circumstances of the project, would be an unbeatable team. Their plan, "Greensward," was accepted in 1858, and work began on the park.

**Enter the park through Scholars' Gate, at the northwest corner of 60th Street and Fifth Avenue.**

**Scholars' Gate**, an opening in the low stone wall along the park's borders, is one of twenty gates in the park, and received its name in the nineteenth century. (1) The park, 843 acres (ultimately extending north to 110th Street), is far

The playful mechanical clock was designed by Andrea Spadini, Edward Coe Embury, and Fernando Texidor.

too large to be toured in a day. So to give you the flavor, we will focus on the southeastern quadrant, with some detours along the way.

**Continue due north on the path.**

For a while you will see only bits of the park with which Vaux and Olmsted had nothing to do. Neither wanted a zoo in the park, but including a "menagerie" was one of many, many compromises they had to make. Not until Robert Moses became parks commissioner in the 1930s did the park get a state-of-the-art zoo. By the 1980s, what was a state-of-the-art small zoo in the 1930s was no longer considered adequate, and Kevin Roche John Dinkeloo and Associates created the present **Central Park Wildlife Center** (1988), a pleasant thing of its kind but not really a part of the story of the park. (2) On the right, opposite the zoo, stands the **Arsenal**. (3) It faces Fifth Avenue at 64th Street and was built in 1847–51 as a storehouse of arms and ammunition. The Arsenal served as the first home (1869–77) of the American Museum of Natural History. In 1934, Robert Moses made it the headquarters of the Parks Department, which it remains to this day.

Vaux's Denesmouth Arch melts into the landscape, unlike more recent park structures (such as the Delacorte Music Clock) that do not seem so site-specific.

**Continue north on the path. Exiting the zoo, look up to view the Delacorte Music Clock.**

The **Delacorte Music Clock** was one of many donations to the park from the book publisher George T. Delacorte. (**4**) Many people find the clock delightful. Delacorte loved mechanical clocks, and this is a public sculpture–sized mechanical clock, in which bronze animals (a bear, a hippopotamus, a penguin, etc.) dance every half-hour to the tunes of nursery rhymes while hammer-wielding monkeys appear to strike the bell. The knock on the clock is that it would be just as delightful no matter where it was placed and that it bears no relationship to the park setting. For some people, it symbolizes the park's sad fate as a kind of dumping ground for well-meaning gifts to the city.

**Continue north just beyond the clock and pass under Denesmouth Arch.**

**Denesmouth Arch** provides our first taste on this walk of the artistry of Calvert Vaux. (**5**) (Vaux had a penchant for romantic names. A "dene" is a valley.)

In Central Park, the schist that is Manhattan's bedrock pokes its head above ground, forming one of the park's characteristic landscape features. The rock descends to more than 100 feet below grade at City Hall Park.

This arch takes the pedestrian under the 65th Street transverse. One of Vaux's many improvements over Viele was in the grade separation of crosstown traffic. While 65th, 79th, 85th, and 97th Streets run latitudinally across the park, they do not block pedestrian passage—seemingly a simple concept, yet ingenious at the time of its implementation. The arch, like all Vaux's park structures and unlike the Delacorte Music Clock, blends—melts—into the landscape. The structure of New Brunswick (Canada, not New Jersey) sandstone bears a Gothic quatrefoil motif. Nature worship and passionate medievalism were closely related in the Romantic Movement, as Central Park attests. Completed in 1859, Denesmouth Arch is one of the earliest structures in Central Park.

**Immediately to the right after Denesmouth Arch is the Tisch Children's Zoo.**

The gate of the **Tisch Children's Zoo**, bearing fertility symbols, was designed by the sculptor Paul Manship (who gave us Rockefeller Center's *Prometheus*, see page 151) and was a gift from Governor and Mrs. Herbert H. Lehman in 1961. **(6)**

**Pass under the next arch, bear left, and continue straight along the path, to come to a high outcropping of schist.**

The land of Central Park was unprepossessing at the time Olmsted commanded an army of Irish laborers in its clearance. Few of the original landscape features remain in the final park design. Among those that do are these outcroppings of Manhattan's bedrock, formed 360 million years ago in the Paleozoic Era. Look at the diagonal striations on the rock, relating the passage through here of the Laurentian Ice Sheet about 20,000 years ago in the late Pleistocene Epoch. While the schist surfaces in this part of the island, it gradually recedes to 112 feet below grade around City Hall in lower Manhattan. In colonial times, the schist was used as a building stone, such as at St. Paul's Chapel on Broadway at Vesey Street. (See pages 20, 21, 38, 39).

**Continue north along the path and pause at the sculpture of the dog, Balto.**

The hero dog **Balto** was rendered in bronze by the leading animalier of his time in New York, Frederick George Richard Roth. (**7**) The statue was dedicated

Frederick George Richard Roth's bronze statue of Balto, the heroic husky that led the sled dog team that brought medicine to save the children of Nome in the 1920s.

in 1925, with Balto, the husky who led the dog team that carried diphtheria serum to the children of stricken Nome during a horrendous blizzard, in attendance (after the dog's death had been erroneously reported by the press). This is very likely the finest dog statue in New York.

**Bear left beyond Balto and pass beneath Vaux's Willowdell Arch.**

**Willowdell Arch** (1861) is actually classical, a segmental arch in sandstone and Philadelphia pressed brick. (8) It carries East Drive, one of three longitudinal park drives. We are now at the line of 67th Street.

**Beyond Willowdell Arch, walk up the hill, bear left along the path, and stop at the southern end of the Mall.**

George Templeton Strong, the nineteenth-century diarist who closely followed the construction of Central Park, called the Mall the one "Versailles-y" part of the park. That is to say, Central Park is a romantic landscape, a place of curvy contours, peekaboo vistas, and seemingly random clumps of trees, all artfully managed to convey the spirit of the countryside. This English tradition—which reached

Calvert Vaux was mainly a Gothic Revivalist, though with Willowdell Arch he resorted to classical forms, albeit using them to highly picturesque effect.

its apogee in the country estates of the late eighteenth and early nineteenth centuries—contrasts with the French classical tradition that we see in Le Nôtre's gardens at Versailles, with their straight allées and sculpted topiary. Both approaches are wholly artificial, though the effects are quite different. The Mall provides Central Park with a formal element that serves to orient the park visitor and acts as a pivot from which different parts of the park may be accessed. Also, the Mall and Bethesda Terrace to which it leads answered the demand that the park offer a place where the upper class could congregate in their splendid carriages, as they did on the Champs-Elysées.

As the one really formal part of the park, the Mall was the only place where Vaux and Olmsted felt statuary was suitable. Basically, everywhere else you see sculpture in the park, it doesn't belong there—at least according to the designers' original intentions. They felt that the definite outlines of sculpture clashed with the blurred-edged naturalism they were after. The Mall readily filled with sculpture, and it is worth perusing it. At the southern end we find a fine statue of William Shakespeare, dedicated in 1872. The sculptor was John Quincy Adams Ward, one of America's most important realists who seldom did "costume pieces" like this but who nonetheless succeeded in giving us an image of the Bard that feels

The canopy of elm branches along the mall evokes a cathedral nave.

absolutely right. Across from it is a statue of Christopher Columbus. The Columbus who surmounts the rostral column in his eponymous Circle is the Italian Columbus. (See pages 212, 213, 237.) The Mall statue is the Spanish Columbus, by the sculptor Jeronimo Suñol, who also did the Columbus monument in Madrid's Plaza de Colón. The date here is 1894.

Entering the Mall, on the left is a seated figure of **Robert Burns**; on the right is **Sir Walter Scott**. In both cases the sculptor was Sir John Steell, probably the leading Scottish sculptor of his generation. The Burns is from 1880. Scott, which derives from Steell's elaborate Scott memorial on Prince's Street in Edinburgh, dates from 1872. A bit farther up the Mall we encounter another "historical romancer," **Fitz-Greene Halleck**, once one of the most famous writers in America. (**9**) His "Marco Bozzaris" was the poetical equivalent of New York's temple-fronted "Grecian" buildings such as Federal Hall National Memorial on Wall Street. The seated figure here dates from 1877 and is the work of James W. A. MacDonald. Its dedication was attended not only by President Rutherford Hayes but also by his entire cabinet.

None of these sculptures is all that exciting, to be sure. A bit southwest of the Mall, however, is J. Q. A. Ward's *Indian Hunter*, a superbly realistic bronze of a young Native American and his hunting dog, on which the details of things like fur and musculature are rendered with heart-stopping precision. (**10**) Ward spent time out west among the Native Americans of the Dakotas, and the date of this sculpture is 1869.

**Continue north along the Mall to where the path widens.**

View a series of smaller bronze sculptures to the west, including *Eagles and Prey* (1850, installed in the park in 1863) by the celebrated French animalier Christophe Fratin; a bust of **Beethoven** (1884) by Henry Baerer; a bust of **Schiller** (1859, the first work of sculpture installed in the park) by C. L. Richter; and a bust of the composer **Victor Herbert** (1927) by Edmond T. Quinn. (**11**)

To the east we find the **Naumburg Bandshell**, built in 1923. (**12**) Once, this "crossing," where the Mall extends east and west in "transepts" before reaching the "chancel" that is Bethesda Terrace, was graveled and planted with trees. To the west, musicians performed on a rustic bandstand, designed by Jacob Wrey Mould (who, with Calvert Vaux, designed the park's structures, including, as we shall see, Bethesda Terrace), while to the east the wisteria-covered pergola provided seating for those

John Quincy Adams Ward was America's leading realist sculptor in the late nineteenth century. His *Indian Hunter* draws from his experience living among and observing Native Americans in the west.

who wished to take in the casual music. Demand arose, however, for formal concerts with seating that would accommodate large audiences. Mould's bandstand was pulled down, along with a bunch of trees, the space was paved over, and the new bandshell went up. Vaux had designed benches surrounding the trees, and these too were removed. The ones you see today are replicas installed by the Central Park Conservancy, a private organization that originated to raise funds for the park and to devise a plan for its rehabilitation following years of neglect and decay.

Lining both sides of the Mall are American elms spreading their branches to create a "cathedral" effect. This is the largest stand of American elms remaining in New York State. This species was virtually obliterated by Dutch elm disease. These particular trees, most of them planted in 1919, are among the most closely guarded trees in America, regularly inspected, pruned, removed, and injected with fungicides to keep disease at bay.

**Continue straight ahead to the terrace at the northern end of the Mall.**

The Mall culminates in one of the most exciting works of architecture in New York. Called **Bethesda Terrace**, this structure has stairs descending into a

Bethesda Terrace leads to a broad plaza, containing Bethesda Fountain and bordering the edge of the lake. On the other side, the Ramble is the park's densely forested area.

broad, covered passageway that in turn gives on to a vast outdoor plaza on the banks of the lake, which separates Bethesda Terrace from the Ramble—the most formal from the most informal parts of the park. (13) This is architecture with no purpose but to give pleasure, and it does that as few if any other built things in the city do.

There are two ways down. South of the transverse are stairs to the covered passageway. They lead you into a room with trompe l'oeil paintings on marble panels lining the walls and exquisite Minton encaustic tiles, recently restored, covering the ceiling. Both paintings and tiles were designed by the brilliant Jacob Wrey Mould.

North of the transverse, on either side of the terrace, are two staircases that lead down in the open. These staircases have side walls of New Brunswick sandstone carved in the most intricate, lush imagery of fruits, flowers, and birds; workmen carved these ornaments to Mould's exacting designs.

Mould was an extraordinary designer. Like Vaux, he was an Englishman. Mould, many believe, had worked for Owen Jones, the author of *The Grammar of Ornament* (1856), an encyclopedia of ornamental patterns extensively consulted by Victorian designers. Jones also had directed the decoration and internal arrangements of Sir Joseph Paxton's Crystal Palace at the Hyde Park exhibition

of 1851, and he designed for the Minton tile company of Stoke-on-Trent, producers of the tiles of Bethesda Terrace. The picturesque Moorish style of the terrace, with its obvious bows to the Alhambra, likely was the work of Vaux, not Mould. Mould was, in the words of the architectural historian David Van Zanten, "the closest thing to a bohemian, many-talented artist New York possessed during the 1850s and 1860s." In addition to being an architect and designer, Mould was a songwriter and translator of opera libretti. Very little is known of Mould's life, though Lucille Gordon, who as a docent for the Central Park Conservancy became fascinated with Mould, has done more than any other scholar to track down details of his background. We know he was born in London and came to New York specifically to design All Souls Unitarian Church, completed in 1855 (and since demolished) on Park Avenue South at 20th Street. That church, and his Trinity Church Parish House on West 25th Street from 1860 (still standing), were two of the most influential works of architecture in Victorian America. Some of Mould's designs at Bethesda Terrace show the distinct influence of Andrea Pisano's fourteenth-century work at the Florence Cathedral. Mould, who knew Dante Gabriel Rossetti, was himself a "pre-Raphaelite" of sorts, and helped mainstream the taste for Italian Primitive art—something to bear in mind the next time you look at Duccio's *Madonna and Child* in the Metropolitan Museum of Art. Later,

One of the longest-running restoration projects in New York finally bore fruit in 2007 with the reinstallation of magnificent Minton tiles designed by Jacob Wrey Mould for the ceiling of the Bethesda Terrace underpass.

Bethesda Terrace and Bethesda Fountain, featuring Emma Stebbins's *Angel of the Waters*, one of New York's iconic images.

Mould, who unlike Olmsted or Vaux was well-connected to the infamous political machine called the Tweed Ring, served as the Parks department's architect, giving Central Park its Sheepfold (now Tavern on the Green) and many other structures.

### Descend the stairs to view *Angel of the Waters*.

Adorning the plaza of Bethesda Terrace is one of New York's most popular sculptures, ***Angel of the Waters***, by Emma Stebbins, set on a fountain designed by Mould and Vaux. (14) In the Gospel of John, the angel stirs the waters of Bethesda, purifying them. The cherubs encircling the statue's base symbolize Health, Purity, Temperance, and Peace. The whole thing was meant to honor New York's accomplishment in constructing the Croton water system, which began operation in 1842. Eleven years later, in acquiring the land for Central Park, the city purposely purchased land surrounding the receiving reservoir for the water system. Many public parks in America were built around preexisting reservoirs. It was a means of ensuring that development did not occur too near the precious sources of water and possibly contaminating them. When Central Park was constructed, it included a new reservoir. In the 1930s, the city drained the original reservoir, and Commissioner Moses created on its site the Great Lawn, behind the Metropolitan Museum of Art.

Some controversy ensued from the choice of Emma Stebbins as the sculptor of the angel. Her brother, Colonel Henry Stebbins, was the president of the Central Park Board of Commissioners. However that may be, she was the first woman ever commissioned to create a public artwork in New York, and she was a major sculptor of her time. She resided in Rome, where several female sculptors formed a circle around the great actress Charlotte Cushman, said to be Stebbins's companion. Henry James, in his book *William Wetmore Story and His Friends*, wrote of these women sculptors, labeling them the White Marmorean Flock. Stebbins also made it into Nathaniel Hawthorne's greatest novel, *The Marble Faun*, as the sculptor Hilda, in a story set among the American expatriate artist community in Rome.

Stebbins's angel stands majestically against a backdrop of water and forest. The water is that of Central Park Lake. Everyone has seen old photographs of skaters on the lake, perhaps with the Dakota apartments in the background. In the nineteenth century, winter was the park's most popular season. Ice skating was at its peak of popularity, and in the colder winters the lake reliably froze over. The Fifth Avenue streetcars would put signs in their front windows alerting New Yorkers to the skating conditions in the park. On freezing days, tens of thousands of skaters took to the lake. Today, it is unsafe to skate on the lake; instead, the Wollman Rink in the southern part of the park and the Lasker Rink and Pool in the northern part serve skaters—though, unfortunately, neither structure is designed in harmony

The Lasker Pool and Rink in the northern part of Central Park was built under Robert Moses, and for many represents the infelicitous incursions inflicted upon the park over the years.

with the surrounding landscape. Across the lake on the right is the **Loeb Boathouse**, where in the summer one of the most pleasant experiences in New York may be had in the fancy Boathouse Restaurant that opens on to the water. **(15)**

The forest belongs to the part of the park called the Ramble. The Ramble is the "Byronic" part of the park, as opposed to the "Wordsworthian." It presents nature in its wilder, less pastoral guise, and is the part of the park where one is likeliest to get lost. The Ramble certainly yields its pleasures, not least to the birds and birders who flock to Central Park, a major stopover on the Great Atlantic Flyway in spring and fall. The Ramble is the last part of the park to be tackled by the Central Park Conservancy, which has been thwarted in its efforts to restore the Ramble to something like its original appearance. The reason some people oppose such restoration is that in the years in which the Ramble has become extremely overgrown, wildlife that had not previously lived there has moved in, and any restoration—any thinning out of the overgrowth—will displace animals from their habitat.

**As you face the lake, bear right along its eastern side onto the pathway that leads to the Boathouse.**

All the water features of Central Park, including the lake, are man-made. In the colder winters of the nineteenth century, the lake reliably and safely froze over. With ice-skating at its peak of popularity, winter was the park's most popular season. The tall building in the distance is the Beresford apartments (Emery Roth, 1929), Central Park West at 81st Street.

The great three-lobed opening of Trefoil Arch reminds us of Calvert Vaux's passionate medievalism, which he had in common with many of his era's artists and intellectuals who sought for an alternative to the harsh industrial city.

From here you will see the tall apartment houses of Central Park West, none of which was there when Central Park was first built. Olmsted and Vaux wished the park to be a respite from the city, an experience of nature. They would not have wanted tall buildings towering over the park. The park user's expectation was that he would leave the city behind.

**Descend the steps on the right that lead down to the vaulted tunnel of Trefoil Arch.**

Designed by Vaux and Mould and built in 1862, **Trefoil Arch** tunnels under East Drive. (**16**) The western entrance is a round arch, but at the other end the opening is a Gothic trefoil. Note also the delicate ironwork railings.

**Pass under Trefoil Arch and bear right. Continue straight along the path to Conservatory Water.**

**Conservatory Water** is so called because it occupies a site specified by Vaux and Olmsted for a greenhouse. (**17**) Instead, the greenhouse was built farther north, around 104th Street, where Commissioner Moses later dismantled it and built the Conservatory Garden. Today, Manhattan, sadly, lacks a public conservatory. The small lake here is famous as the place where children play with their model boats—and as the scene of a dramatic model-boat race in E. B. White's classic *Stuart Little*. The structure on the east side of the water is the Kerbs Model Boathouse from 1954, designed by architect Aymar Embury II.

**Turn north on the path that runs along the west side of Conservatory Water.**

The area surrounding the Conservatory Water is brilliant in the spring. To the north and west of the water, cherry trees blossom forth in pink and white, the mulberry bushes in front of the boathouse blossom white, daffodils thrive on Pilgrim Hill to the south of the water, and the leaves of the Norway maples are a lovely reddish hue. To the west of the water is Georg Lober's 1956 bronze caricatural seated figure of Hans Christian Andersen, while to the north of the water is José de Creeft's *Alice in Wonderland* group from 1959, another gift of George T. Delacorte. (18) No one thinks these are not lovely works of their kind, but some question whether they really belong in a park to which they bear no aes-

*Alice in Wonderland*, a gift of publisher George T. Delacorte, whom sculptor José de Creeft affectionately caricatures as the Mad Hatter.

thetic relation. When someone once asked former Curator of Central Park Henry Hope Reed if it wasn't true that children loved these sculptures, Reed replied, "Children love the park anyway."

**Continue due north on the path to the west of the Alice in Wonderland group to Glade Arch.**

This path takes you through the Glade, from about 75th to about 78th Streets. Vaux's **Glade Arch** runs under an easterly spur of East Drive. (**19**) For this arch, Vaux chose a stately classical design, with rusticated voussoirs and classical balustrades, deliberately evoking the placement of classical structures in romantic settings by British landscape gardeners such as Lancelot "Capability" Brown, who in turn evoked the landscape paintings of Claude Lorrain, who in turn evoked the imagery of Virgil—"The whole thing was brought home in luggage from the grand tour," as Tom Stoppard says in his play *Arcadia*.

**Immediately past Glade Arch on the left is Cedar Hill. Continue along the path to the right of the hill. Cross the 79th Street transverse.**

Beyond Glade Arch we encounter **Cedar Hill** (**20**), then the mammoth edifice of the **Metropolitan Museum of Art.** (**21**) Vaux and Mould's original museum building was a redbrick Gothic Revival structure of modest scale. An exterior wall of the original building, which opened in 1880, is visible today inside the museum's Lehman Wing. In the 1890s, Richard Morris Hunt designed a classical Fifth Avenue facade for the museum, which was later extended south and north by McKim, Mead & White. A major expansion of the museum in the 1970s and 1980s, designed by Kevin Roche John Dinkeloo and Associates, controversially backed up into the park. Clockwise from the southeast, we see the Michael C. Rockefeller Wing for Primitive Art, from 1981; the Lila Acheson Wallace Wing, 1986; the pyramid-topped Lehman Wing (1975); the American Wing, 1980; and the Sackler Wing for the Temple of Dendur, 1979.

**Pass over the 79th Street transverse and bear left along the path that runs behind the museum to Greywacke Arch.**

**Greywacke Arch** of 1861–63 was designed by Mould in a Moorish style in gray sandstone, called North River greywacke, and Passaic River brownstone. (**22**) To many, it is the most delicious of the park's arches, especially for its beautiful iron railings. Beyond it and to the right stands, on a hill reached by steps, one of the

The Lehman Wing of the Metropolitan Museum of Art is one of the museum's modern extensions into the park. The pyramidal form is a bow to the nearby Obelisk.

most remarkable objects in New York: the **Obelisk**, sometimes (inaccurately) called "Cleopatra's Needle." **(23)**

**Pass beneath Greywacke Arch and take the path on the right that leads to the staircase to the Obelisk.**

Ancient Egyptian obelisks are very rare, and it's amazing that one should be on a hill in Central Park. This pink granite obelisk, 69 feet high, is from the fifteenth century BC, when it was erected by Pharaoh Thutmose III at the Temple of Tum at Heliopolis, the center of worship of the sun god. It was moved in 12 BC to Alexandria. In 1869, in commemoration of the opening of the Suez Canal, the khedive of Egypt gave an obelisk to London (which placed it on the Victoria Embankment) and one to New York. We got it here—with much difficulty—in 1881, and it's been on this hill ever since. Today, only twenty-two such obelisks exist: one here, one in London, one in Paris, one in Istanbul, five in Egypt, and thirteen in Rome. Paris erected the thirteenth-century BC Luxor obelisk on the Place de la Concorde in 1836. It has been said that Napoleon had his eye on the obelisk now in Central Park, but his savants told him it was too deteriorated. There has been much controversy over whether the obelisk here has been properly cared for, with some people claiming that it has decayed more in the century and a quarter it's been in New York than it had in nearly two millennia prior to that. That's nonsense. What isn't nonsense is that not one in a thousand—if that many—New Yorkers realizes this is one of the most important objects in the Western Hemisphere. One problem I have had with the Obelisk is its placement here. In Rome and Paris, obelisks are used as place-making objects in an urbanistic context, whereas in Central Park the Obelisk, however remarkable a thing it is in itself, seems unanchored—another thing that would be as good as or better than it is if it were placed elsewhere than in the park. The best place from which to view the Obelisk, it turns out, may be from inside the museum's Petrie European Sculpture Court, where Roche Dinkeloo framed the view of the Obelisk so that it lines up on an axis—the only vantage point from which it does.

We've seen but a slice of Central Park. I think the park has shown greater tolerances in its uses than anyone could have foreseen, and we must credit some of that to Robert Moses. On the other hand, I think we would do well—as I think

Calvert Vaux's picturesque Greywacke Arch, behind the Metropolitan Museum of Art, features a beautiful iron railing. Ironwork was a special interest of Vaux's.

The Obelisk is the only ancient Egyptian obelisk in the Western Hemisphere. This gift from the khedive of Egypt is one of the city's most valuable cultural artifacts.

we shall—going forward not to deviate any further from, and as much as possible to restore, the vision of Calvert Vaux. After all, we could use some rest and relaxation in New York in the twenty-first century.

**Leaving**

**By Subway:** 6 at 77th Street; B, C at 81st Street–Museum of Natural History
**By Bus:** M79

## Suggested Reading

*Central Park, An American Masterpiece: A Comprehensive History of the Nation's First Urban Park*, by Sara Cedar Miller. Harry N. Abrams, Inc., in association with the Central Park Conservancy, 2003. A superb illustrated history that makes use of all the latest research and that brings the reader up to date on the heroic efforts of the Central Park Conservancy to restore the park.

*Central Park – Prospect Park: A New Perspective*, by M. M. Graff. Greensward Foundation, Inc., 1985. A peppery and provocative study of the parks by a staunch advocate of Calvert Vaux's importance over that of Frederick Law Olmsted.

*Central Park: A History and a Guide*, by Henry Hope Reed and Sophia Duckworth. Clarkson N. Potter, Inc., 1967. A sprightly history and tour of the park from the viewpoint of a highly refined aesthetic sensibility, cowritten by the onetime curator of Central Park.

*Country, Park & City: The Architecture and Life of Calvert Vaux*, by Francis R. Kowsky. Oxford University Press, 1998. An excellent biography of the brilliant English architect who did so much for New York City.

*Robert Moses and the Modern City: The Transformation of New York*, by Hillary Ballon and Kenneth Jackson, 2007. A magnificent collection of essays by leading scholars reconsidering the impact of "master builder" Robert Moses on New York's cityscape, not least on the city's parks.

*The Park and the People: A History of Central Park*, by Roy Rosenzweig and Elizabeth Blackmar. Cornell University Press, 1992. The standard academic work on the subject, with more of an emphasis on social and political history than on architectural history.

# 10. Harlem Haven

## Hamilton Heights

**FRANCIS MORRONE**

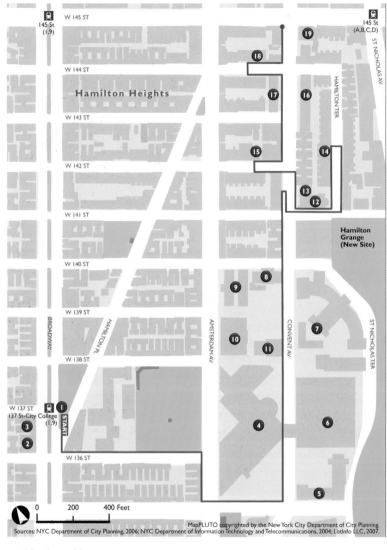

MapPLUTO copyrighted by the New York City Department of City Planning.
Sources: NYC Department of City Planning, 2006; NYC Department of Information Technology and Telecommunications, 2004; LotInfo LLC, 2007.

## Harlem Haven: Hamilton Heights

1  IRT subway station at 137th
   Street/City College
2  Saxonia
3  Leslie Court
4  CCNY North Academic
   Center
5  Asa Philip Randolph High
   School
6  Marshak Hall

7  Shepard Hall
8  Baskerville Hall
9  Compton-Goethals Hall
10 Harris Hall
11 Wingate Hall
12 St. Luke's Episcopal Church
13 Hamilton Grange National
   Memorial
14 4–30 Hamilton Terrace

15 Our Lady of Lourdes
16 311–339 Convent Avenue
17 320–328 Convent Avenue
18 453–467 West 144th Street
19 Convent Avenue Baptist
   Church

**By Subway:** I to 137th Street / City College
**By Bus:** M4, M5, M11

Hamilton Heights is part of the greater Upper West Side that remained largely rural until the late nineteenth century. First the Ninth Avenue elevated railway, then the IRT subway, brought building booms to all the West Side, not least to western Harlem, where we find Hamilton Heights. Speculative overbuilding of upper Manhattan created an unprecedented opportunity for New York's—and America's—African Americans. The enterprising African-American real estate agent Philip A. Payton Jr. established an office on West 134th Street in 1903, at a time when most of Harlem was still new. He himself moved with his wife to an 1887 house at 13 West 131st Street in 1903. By 1915, that block, between Fifth Avenue and Malcolm X Boulevard, was occupied completely by African-American families. What's notable in all this may be seen in an advertisement Payton ran in *The New York Age*:

> Colored Tenants, Attention! After much effort I am now able to offer to my people for rent [homes] of a class never before rented to our people.

The segregation of African Americans meant that even successful professionals and entrepreneurs had no choice but to live in poor areas, such as Hell's Kitchen in west Midtown. The opening of Harlem's outstanding housing stock to African Americans afforded them access to better, comelier, more commodious, and more modern housing than they had ever enjoyed—ever—in their history in America. This is the background to the cultural efflorescence we call the Harlem Renaissance, when in the 1920s—poverty and social hardships notwithstanding—an optimism prevailed. Though the Great Depression, and the post–World War II mass migration of southern blacks to New York in quest of factory jobs that were fast disappearing, dented that optimism, it has not ceased to be the case that Harlem is the undisputed capital of black America. And as African Americans have contributed so much to American culture, then it is that so much of American culture is deeply rooted in the streets, row houses, apartments, and churches of Harlem. For me, one especially interesting part of Harlem is Hamilton Heights.

## We will begin our tour on Broadway at 137th Street, at the station of the West Side IRT.

The **137th Street/City College IRT station** opened in 1904, part of the city's first subway line. (**1**) At the time, City College's Hamilton Heights campus was under construction—as was much of the West Side. An earlier speculative boom had occurred in the 1880s and 1890s following the introduction of elevated train service along Ninth (Columbus) Avenue. But when the Interborough Rapid Transit Company opened its subterranean railroad under Broadway in 1904, speculation turned to mania, as one apartment house after another came to Broadway, forming the earliest apartment house neighborhood in America. Note just the ones within a block of the subway station. At the northwest corner of Broadway and 136th Street stands the **Saxonia**, 601 West 136th Street, from 1906–7, designed by Neville & Bagge, one of the pioneering firms that helped define the vernacular style of the Manhattan apartment building. (**2**) Immediately to its north, at 602 West 137th Street, Emery Roth's **Leslie Court** dates from 1907. (**3**) Roth is one of the two or three most renowned apartment-house architects in New York history. He also designed the Cromwell, at the northwest corner of 137th, built in 1906–7. The Royal Arms, at the southwest corner of 138th, dates from 1906 and was designed by Thain & Thain. Neville & Bagge gave us the 1906 building on the west side of Broadway between 138th and 139th Streets. All these apartment buildings arrived in the immediate wake of the opening of the IRT, and all are six- or seven-story elevator buildings.

The Saxonia is an exceptionally handsome building. Its first story on Broadway is buried in a jumble of storefronts; on 136th Street, though, it is rusticated limestone. The remaining five stories are faced in brick, but with the windows beautifully framed in lushly ornamented terra-cotta. At the top story, the windows terminate in segmental arches, and the whole is topped by a strong cornice. The facades are carefully composed, richly ornamented, and dignified; everything about them makes visual sense, and the patterns employed are repeatable. This is urban architecture at its unassuming best. Thomas Neville and George Bagge began their partnership in 1892 as designers of row houses. Later on this walk,

Architects Neville & Bagge, in buildings such as the Saxonia, were among the pioneers in developing an appropriate style for the Manhattan apartment house. Such buildings form the rich background fabric of the city.

we will see excellent examples of their row-house work. By the turn of the century, row-house construction ground to a halt in Manhattan, and Neville & Bagge turned to apartment houses. The partnership lasted until 1917. They were astonishingly prolific: Between 1900 and 1917, reports Christopher Gray of the *New York Times*, they filed plans for 401 new buildings in New York City. In works like the Saxonia, or the 12-story Dorchester (1908) on Riverside Drive at 85th Street, they helped rationalize and conventionalize the form of the New York apartment house. Previously, apartment-house designs had been all over the place, as architects tried more than anything to distinguish their buildings from the tenements of the poor. The Tenement House Act of 1901, which brought tenements more in line with middle-class apartment houses, and the IRT of 1904, which helped spur the rapid build-out of apartment houses, requiring the reuse and repetition of conventional patterns (just as had happened with row houses), led to the "classic" New York apartment building, perfectly exemplified by the works of Neville & Bagge.

Leslie Court, next to the Saxonia, was one of the early apartment buildings by Emery Roth, who later designed twin-towered classics on Central Park West.

Emery Roth's Leslie Court, abutting the Saxonia to the north, has some spectacular terra-cotta ornamentation. The way the 137th Street corner is visually reinforced in terra-cotta is both eye-catching and unexpected. Roth's Cromwell, across 137th Street, is another beauty, with its rusticated brickwork, ornamental panels, oriels, and broken cornice. To the north of the Cromwell, the Royal Arms by Thain & Thain shows that the basic form laid down in the first decade of the twentieth century need not foreclose on eccentric touches. The handling of the fluted pilasters, rising three stories from high bases, and especially the pilasters joining at the corner to seem to form a solid column embedded in the facade, are highly unusual.

It would be tempting just to tour the apartment houses of Broadway, which in virtually any stretch of the great boulevard offer visual treats. But we will try to get a sense of Hamilton Heights as a whole.

**Proceed south to 136th Street and turn east one block to Amsterdam Avenue. Here we come to the campus of City College of New York (CCNY).**

City College's campus divides into the South Campus, bounded by 130th and 135th Streets and Amsterdam Avenue and St. Nicholas Terrace, and the North Campus, bounded by 135th and 141st Streets and Amsterdam Avenue and St. Nicholas Terrace. We will focus on the North Campus, the most historic part of City College.

City College began as the Free Academy of the City of New York in 1847. Until its 1907 move to Hamilton Heights, City College was located on Lexington Avenue at 23rd Street, in a building designed by James Renwick Jr. (It is no longer standing.) Renwick's Gothic design established an image for City College, which wished to continue its medieval associations when it hired George B. Post, one of New York's greatest architects of all time, to design the new campus uptown, ground for which was broken in 1903, just before the IRT opened.

At 136th Street, the first building we encounter is the gigantic **North Academic Center**, an irregularly shaped complex that at its widest dimensions extends all the way from 135th to 138th Streets and from Amsterdam to Convent Avenues. (**4**) It was designed by John Carl Warnecke & Associates and built in 1983. It's a sleek affair of jutting angles, curving corners, and banded windows. No doubt it answered to very complicated program requirements, but it neither relates in a meaningful way to the college's glorious older campus nor inspires any affection on its own. The North Academic Center was built on the site of City College's 6,000-seat Lewisohn Stadium, arguably the noblest stadium in New York, designed by Arnold W. Brunner and built in 1915.

**Walk south to 135th Street and then continue east.**

On the north side of 135th Street between Convent Avenue and St. Nicholas Terrace stands **Asa Philip Randolph High School**, one among the city's many handsome public school buildings designed by C. B. J. Snyder. (**5**) Here, the Gothic style was meant to harmonize with the old City College buildings. Alas, between the high school and the old buildings two large modernist buildings have intervened, destroying any relationship that might once have existed.

**Turn north along the west side of Convent Avenue. To the north of the high school, extending from 136th to 138th Streets, stands Marshak Hall, from 1971, by Skidmore, Owings & Merrill.**

One wonders at the architects' total lack of concern for the visual relationship between the new and the old. A new building need not be in the style of the old to relate pleasingly. But in 1971 with **Marshak Hall** (**6**)—and again with

North Academic Center in 1983—such a relationship simply was of no concern to the architects. It wasn't just at City College but at schools all across the country that such interventions, from the 1950s on, destroyed campuses.

**Continue north to 138th Street.**

With North Academic Center and Marshak Hall at your back, City College comes true. **Shepard Hall,** facing the northeast corner of Convent Avenue and 138th Street, is one of the finest buildings in New York and one of the finest collegiate buildings in America. (**7**) The part pointing to the corner is like the apse of a great cathedral, set diagonally on its site in a northeast-southwest orientation. The "transept" wings curve dramatically in western and southern directions. The form and siting of Shepard Hall (also known as the Main Building) were suggested by the almost triangular plot, made so by the sharp northwestern bend of St. Nicholas Terrace between the line of 139th Street and 140th Street. The 138th Street gateway to the Shepard Hall site, called the George Washington Gate, is a triple portal, with great stone and terra-cotta arches, in the Gothic style, flanking an exquisite arched span of filigreed ironwork. This gateway frames one view of Shepard Hall.

George B. Post was hired by City College in 1897 to design its new campus. Construction commenced in 1903, and between then and 1907 five Post-designed buildings rose between 138th and 140th Streets and Amsterdam Avenue and St. Nicholas Terrace, or what is today the northernmost part of the North Campus. The other four buildings are to the west of Convent Avenue, while Shepard Hall, to the east of Convent, appears to be nearly as large as the other four combined. Post, a native New Yorker, was born in 1837. He attended New York University and studied in its great Collegiate Gothic building facing Washington Square. After graduating in 1858 with a degree in civil engineering, he went to work in the office/atelier of Richard Morris Hunt, who in that year was only five years removed from his eight-year stint in Paris, where he had been the first American to study architecture at the École des Beaux-Arts—something Post never did, though Hunt strove to bring Beaux-Arts–style training to New York.

After the Civil War, in which he served as a colonel, Post formed his own firm in 1867. In 1870–75 he designed the remarkable Williamsburgh Savings Bank on Broadway at Driggs Avenue in Brooklyn. Its grand classical style was unusual for New York buildings in the 1870s and would not in fact become popular until the 1890s. On the strength of that building, Post won the 1878 competition for the design of the Long Island (now Brooklyn) Historical Society in Brooklyn Heights,

Shepard Hall at City College is the ultimate in Collegiate Gothic, facing Convent Avenue with a bold form reminiscent of the apse of a medieval cathedral.

completed in 1881. In my opinion, if Post had designed nothing but the double-height library in that building and Shepard Hall he would still have to be ranked among the great New York architects. But he designed so much more, including the tragically demolished Produce Exchange (1881–84) at 2 Broadway.

St. Nicholas Terrace is a great, high bluff of Manhattan schist looking out over the Harlem plain. To save money, City College chose to use as the campus's principal building stone the very schist blasted away to make way for the campus. At that time, schist was not commonly used as a building stone. In colonial times it was used for St. Paul's Chapel on Broadway between Fulton and Vesey Streets (see pages 21, 22, 39) and for the Van Cortlandt house at Broadway and 242nd Street in Van Cortlandt Park in the Bronx, as well as for other buildings. It was also occasionally used since then, for example in the original buildings in Central Park, which is also famous for its high outcroppings of this Manhattan bedrock. It wasn't a fashionable stone in 1903, yet the decision to use it—and Post's mating of the dark stone with a bright white terra-cotta (produced by the Perth Amboy Terra Cotta Company)—proved inspired. As the architectural historian Sarah Bradford Landau points out in her excellent book *George B. Post, Architect* (1998), the leading architecture critic of the day, Montgomery Schuyler, felt the contrast between the

George B. Post took the schist of the bluff atop which Shepard Hall stands and crafted an exquisite image of learning—one of the most beautiful sights in New York.

281

stone and the terra-cotta to be jarring and to diminish the otherwise excellent picturesque design. Yet I, for one, find the effect exciting. Shepard Hall is a wondrous confection of stepped buttresses, finialed towers, crenellated parapets, and slit-like windows, with gloriously lacy terra-cotta outlines. The turrets defining the corners of the square towers rise to heart-meltingly filigreed cupolas. Atop its bluff, Shepard Hall pulls no punches in packing a picturesque wallop that perhaps no other Manhattan building can claim.

Lewis Mumford, the brilliant critic who was notably averse to "revival" styles in architecture, attended City College as a night student. Here is what he said in his autobiography *Sketches from Life* (1982):

> . . . the college buildings, in their dark stone masses and white terra-cotta quoins and moldings, rising like a collection of crystals above the formless rocks of the hill. Below, the plains of Harlem spread a vapor of light beneath the twinkle and flood of a large beer sign. The Gothic architecture of the main building, which followed the curve of the

George B. Post's brilliant use of the Gothic style made the smokestack of Compton Hall, the campus power plant, into a dramatic skyline element.

The Collegiate Gothic style sought to identify the modern college experience with the monastic learning of the Middle Ages. This "grotesque" at Compton-Goethals Hall shows how the theme was carried through all the details of the building.

escarpment and dominated it with the tower of the Great Hall, did magnificent justice to its setting. In the afterglow, or on a dark night, these buildings could awaken nostalgic tremors as easily as might those of Trinity or Magdalen.

Not only is that one of the most beautiful passages ever written about New York buildings, but it attests to the unique power of architecture to inspire affection—"nostalgic tremors"—even after seventy or so years, which is the distance between Mumford's student years and when he wrote his autobiography. Some may say this is stage-set architecture. So? Aren't plays art?

## Continue north on Convent Avenue and pause just before 140th Street, facing west, to view the other four Post buildings.

At the southwest corner of Convent Avenue and 140th Street stands **Baskerville Hall**, one of Post's original City College buildings. (**8**) To its west is Post's **Compton Hall**, adjoined by **Goethals Hall**, built in 1930 by George B. Post & Sons. (**9**) (Post's firm took that name in 1904. Post died in 1913, but the firm continued for a number of years.) Compton Hall was originally known as the Mechanical Arts Building and housed the campus power plant. It's a brilliant building. For Post there was no contradiction between dressing his buildings in medieval garb and forthrightly expressing the mechanical function of a power plant. He turned the central smokestack into a powerfully picturesque skyline element. To the south of Compton-Goethals stands Post's **Harris Hall,** (**10**) while to its east on 138th Street stands Post's **Wingate Hall.** (**11**)

George B. Post's
buildings for City
College made
use of the dark
schist quarried
on the site,
contrasted with
snowy terra-
cotta.

285

R. H. Robertson's St. Luke's Episcopal Church, on Convent Avenue, is a bold "Richardsonian Romanesque" building that sidles elegantly toward St. Nicholas Avenue.

**Let's now leave City College and explore residential and ecclesiastical Hamilton Heights. Continue north along Convent Avenue and pause on the northwest corner of 141st Street.**

One block north of Shepard Hall stands **St. Luke's Episcopal Church**, designed by R. H. Robertson and built in 1892–95. **(12)** The congregation of this Episcopal parish originated in Greenwich Village in the 1820s, at the church now known as St. Luke in the Fields, on Hudson Street at Grove Street. The elite congregation—the founders of which included Clement Clarke Moore, the famous scholar and putative author of the poem "A Visit from St. Nicholas"—moved uptown to Hamilton Heights in 1889 and held its first service in the Alexander Hamilton house (see below), which St. Luke's had just moved south on Convent Avenue from 143rd to 141st Streets to make way for a profitable row-house development. The architect of the new church, R. H. Robertson, was known for his "Richardsonian Romanesque" designs. He was one of many 1880s acolytes of the Boston-based architect Henry Hobson Richardson, whose personal adaptation of the medieval Romanesque struck many as a style perfectly suited to the violently expanding nation of the 1880s. Here, Robertson, working with a limited budget, created a beautiful church, compact like a fireplug or a clenched fist, of rock-faced sandstone ashlar, with tightly massed triple-arched windows, broad red-tiled roofs, and a simple, strong, arched and gabled entrance on Convent Avenue. Of special note are the strong open arcades and the rhythmical way Robertson lets the church's mass sidle down the slope toward Hamilton Terrace. Be sure to walk around to the rear to see the powerful rounded apse. Particularly impressive is how Robertson, whose budget curtailed his use of ornament, varied his treatment of the ashlar to give expressive force to the building's masses.

Robertson employed much the same formal vocabulary in his contemporaneous American Tract Society Building on Park Row, one of the earliest steel-framed skyscrapers in New York. (See also pages 64, 65.)

## Continue a few paces north on Convent Avenue.

Across 141st Street from the church in St. Nicholas Park, opposite Hamilton Terrace, stands **Hamilton Grange National Memorial**, the onetime country home of Alexander Hamilton. (**13**) The house, designed by John McComb Jr., was completed in 1802. At the time, Hamilton, at forty-five years old, had his glory years as a public man behind him. He wanted a country place (it was the only residence he ever owned) where he might write his memoirs. At the time, this part of Manhattan was way out in the country. The island had not yet been platted into its gridiron of streets, much less had the streets been cut through. Alas for Hamilton! He got embroiled in the New York gubernatorial race of 1804, commenting to the newspapers about his distaste for one of the candidates, Aaron Burr, who was at the time the vice president of the United States. As rival lawyers, bankers, and politicians, the two men's mutual enmity reached a tragic climax when Burr challenged Hamilton to a duel. On July 11, in a field in Weehawken, New Jersey, across the Hudson from the future site of West 42nd Street, Burr shot and killed Hamilton. It is one of only two recorded instances of a sitting vice president of the United States shooting someone.

John McComb Jr. (1763–1853), credited with the design of Hamilton's home, was one of the earliest professional architects in New York. The Ulsterman's credits include Castle Clinton, in Battery Park, and the interior of City Hall. His greatest work was St. John's Church (1803), on Varick Street, facing St. John's Square, the elegant residential square, a model for Gramercy Park, that was replaced by Commodore Vanderbilt's freight terminal (in its turn replaced by the exit rotary of the Holland Tunnel). In 1918, amid vociferous protests, St. John's Church was pulled down.

Hamilton Grange originally stood on Convent Avenue at 143rd Street. When St. Luke's Church purchased property up here in the 1880s, it included the grange. To make way for a row house development, the church moved Hamilton Grange to Convent Avenue at 141st Street. For many years, preservationists had protested that the house, hemmed in on three sides with only one visible facade and no grounds around it, gave no sense of what it must have been like when Hamilton lived in it. The house, which operates as a historic house museum administered by the National Park Service, was moved to nearby St. Nicholas Park in the summer of 2008. The house now enjoys full visibility and gives off a sense of being a country house.

Across Convent Avenue from the former site of Hamilton Grange is a row of seven houses designed by Henri Fouchaux and built in 1899–1902. This exciting neo-Renaissance row has some of the most elaborate window enframements you'll see in New York, with pediments (triangular and rounded), keystones, brackets, and deeply projecting sills. There are also oculi, cartouches, and colonnettes galore. Even the chimneys add to the palatial effect. Fouchaux, who is well represented in Hamilton Heights, was an adventuresome architect whose name might be better known had he not died at age fifty-four in 1910.

Alexander Hamilton, New York's own among the Founding Fathers, did not have the enjoyment of his 1802 country house, the Grange, for long before he was shot by Aaron Burr in 1804. In an exacting move in June 2008, the 298-ton-Hamilton Grange National memorial was moved to nearby St. Nicholas Park.

Hamilton Terrace is a three-block-long enclave delectably located just north of the original campus of City College.

Before continuing up Convent Avenue, it's good to look in on Hamilton Terrace, a three-block-long north-south street to the east of Convent and the west of St. Nicholas Terrace.

**Return to 141st Street, turn east for one block, and then proceed north along Hamilton Terrace.**

Hamilton Terrace is a handsome enclave. The houses aren't as fine as on Convent Avenue, but that's more than compensated for by the dramatic way in which Hamilton Terrace lies on the axis of City College's Shepard Hall—the "cathedral" of learning looming over the tranquil neighborhood as in an idealized medieval town. At 19 Hamilton Terrace stands a tan-brick modernist apartment house made attractive by its broad curving balconies with pipe railings, a sort of "Moderne" touch as one might expect from an apartment house built in 1948–51. The architect, Vertner Woodson Tandy, who died while the building was under construction, was the first African American to become a registered architect in New York State. Tandy's masterpiece, St. Philip's Episcopal Church (1910–11), on 134th Street at Adam Clayton Powell Jr. Boulevard, is not far from here and is

well worth a visit, both for its architecture and for its historic associations with
W. E. B. Du Bois, Langston Hughes, and Thurgood Marshall, all of whom attended
services there.

Perhaps the best houses on Hamilton Terrace are the ones in the 14-house
row at numbers **4–30**. (**14**) These were designed by Neville & Bagge and built in
1898. It's a beautifully composed row, and the houses boast fine brickwork and
nicely executed, very precise classical devices. We met this firm near the beginning of our walk, when we saw their Saxonia apartments on Broadway. Neville &
Bagge were renowned for their apartment houses but began as row-house architects, switching to apartments when the row-house market dried up. The firm
also designed the eccentric, but finely crafted, mansarded house at 72 Hamilton
Terrace, built in 1897. Perhaps because it specialized in workaday speculative commissions, Neville & Bagge has never received its due as one of the outstanding
firms that truly contributed to the quality of Manhattan's urban fabric in the late

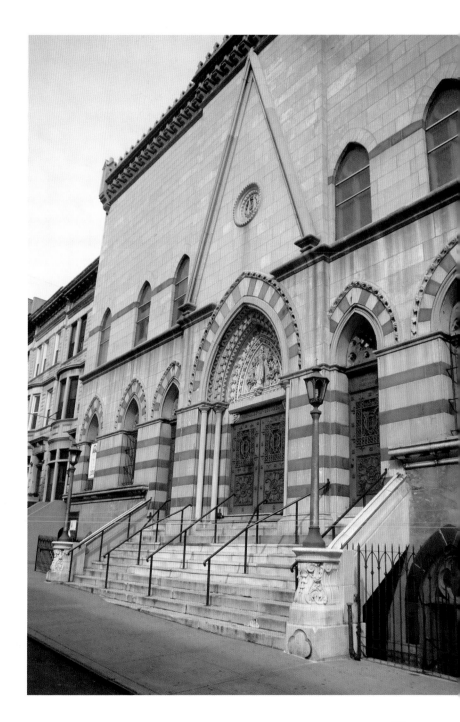

nineteenth and early twentieth centuries. Most of the houses on Hamilton Terrace date from the 1890s. An exception is the handsome Georgian Revival town house at number 51, built in 1909 and designed by Schwartz & Gross—like Neville & Bagge, a firm known for its speculative apartment houses.

**Return to Convent Avenue and proceed north to 142nd Street. Cross the avenue and proceed midblock, pausing on the south side of the street.**

On the north side of 142nd Street between Convent and Amsterdam Avenues stands one of the most unusual churches in New York, **Our Lady of Lourdes**, designed (or assembled) by the O'Reilly Brothers and built in 1902–4. (**15**) Most of the facade was salvaged from one of the greatest New York buildings ever to be torn down, the National Academy of Design, which stood on Park Avenue South at 24th Street from 1863 to 1900. The academy was designed by Peter B. Wight, one of the principal American acolytes of the English writer John Ruskin, and was in the characteristically "Ruskinian" Gothic style of fifteenth-century Venice. Inside the church, the architects, the O'Reilly Brothers, recycled bits—including stained-glass windows—that were removed from the east end of St. Patrick's Cathedral, on Fifth Avenue, when construction began on the Lady Chapel in 1901. While it's not exactly a substitute for preservation, there is something deeply touching about these substantial parts of superannuated structures making their way to the newest neighborhood uptown.

**Return to Convent Avenue and continue walking north to 144th Street.**

The east side of Convent Avenue between the line of 143rd and 144th Streets (143rd Street does not go through between Convent and Bradhurst Avenues) belongs to an architect named Adolph Hoak, whose picturesque row houses form a highly pleasing ensemble, notable for their purposely varied styles, materials, and roofline treatments. The fifteen houses, **311–339**, were built in 1887–90 by a realtor named Jacob D. Butler. (**16**) The house at 339, terminating the row at the southeast corner of 144th Street, is a splendid Romanesque Revival mansion with a great, swelling corner tower enhanced by densely clustered, beautifully proportioned, vertically elongated windows with curving glass panes.

On the west side of Convent Avenue, the five houses at **320–328** were designed by an architect named Horace Hartwell and built in 1890. (**17**) They form a powerfully picturesque row with varied and elaborate gables. The corner house at 320 has a big, rounded corner tower. At 324, the top floor has a broad window within a boldly scaled chamfered arch and spandrels filled with lacy, Sullivanesque terra-cotta ornamentation. A giant, swelling, two-story bay marks 328. The four houses at 330 to 336 date from 1890–92 and were designed by an architect named Robert Dry. They use brick and stone to simulate the half-timbering of Tudor architecture. The end house, at 336, is wonderful, with its great, big, round corner tower and an exuberant conical roof. The way it complements the towered house across the avenue at 339 (see above) makes for one of the urbanistic highlights of upper Manhattan.

**Turn west along the south side of 144th Street.**

The houses at **453–467 West 144th Street** date from 1886–90 and were designed by William E. Mowbray. (18) Mowbray preceded Robert Dry (see above) in using brick with stone bands to simulate Tudor-style half-timbering. The picturesque effect is especially notable at 457, where horizontal stone bands of the "half-timbering" intersect the lines of a centrally placed second-floor Palladian window, and where the house is topped off by a fanciful curving gable. I doubt there is any more delirious sequence of gables in Manhattan than we find in this row. The ground floor of number 463 is recessed behind a giant arch, forming an open porch, while the rest of the house above it rises in a kind of oozy rounded mass. These houses belong very much to the period of the Queen Anne style. Mowbray is another architect who deserves to be better known than he is. The outstanding *AIA Guide to New York City* lists only one building by him—an apartment house on the Upper East Side. Yet he also designed Oscar Hammerstein's Manhattan Opera House (1906) as well as several wonderful houses in Harlem. Be sure to look at the row across the street at 468 to 474, austerely picturesque houses with bold stoop treatments and porches, designed by Harvey Page and built in 1887–89.

**Return to Convent Avenue and continue north to the southwest corner of 145th Street.**

At the southeast corner of 145th Street stands the very fine Gothic Revival **Convent Avenue Baptist Church**, built in 1897–99. (19) The architects, Lamb & Rich, created a simple church that, with its sequence of gables on 145th Street, presents a spiky skyline from which a square, crenellated tower rises at the corner with just enough force to anchor the intersection. The stone of the facades is admirably handled, and the church works, if not with the bravura manner of

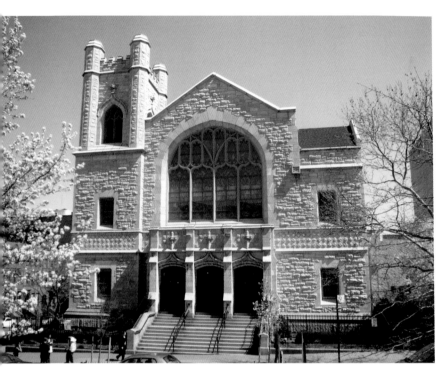

Lamb & Rich's elegantly designed Convent Avenue Baptist Church was the scene of the Rev. Dr. Martin Luther King Jr.'s last public appearance in New York.

George B. Post's buildings at City College, then nonetheless efficiently and handsomely to form a fine Gothic frame for Hamilton Heights, where all manner of buildings harmonize in one of the most delightful enclaves in Manhattan.

Historically, too, there is something special. Alexander Hamilton lived here. A bit north in Sugar Hill Duke Ellington, W. E. B. Du Bois, Thurgood Marshall, Walter White, and many other twentieth-century notables once resided. Just around the corner from Convent Avenue Baptist Church, at 749 St. Nicholas Avenue, between 147th and 148th Streets, lived Ralph Ellison from 1945 to 1953 when he wrote *Invisible Man*. Not least, Convent Avenue Baptist Church was the scene of the Rev. Dr. Martin Luther King Jr.'s last public appearance in New York, on March 26, 1968, only a few days before he was assassinated in Memphis. Add in the architecture of George B. Post, Henri Fouchaux, William E. Mowbray, and Neville & Bagge, and I don't think you can ask for many more artistic or historical resonances from a neighborhood.

Leaving

**By Subway:** 1 at 145th Street; A, C, B, D at 145th Street
**By Bus:** M4, M5, M3

# Suggested Reading

*Alexander Hamilton, American*, by Richard Brookhiser. Free Press, 1999. The best brief life of "America's first prime minister."

*City on a Hill: Testing the American Dream at City College*, by James Traub. Addison-Wesley, 1994. A book that examines the significance of City College as a New York and an American institution.

*George B. Post, Architect*, by Sarah Bradford Landau. Monacelli Press, 1998. The first, and the definitive, monograph on the great New York architect who gave us the beautiful original part of the City College campus.

*Harlem, Lost and Found: An Architectural and Social History, 1765–1915*, by Michael Henry Adams. Monacelli Press, 2002. The wonders of Harlem (including Hamilton Heights) architecture and history pictured and described in a volume that is a true labor of love.

*Touring Historic Harlem: Four Walks in Northern Manhattan*, by Andrew S. Dolkart and Gretchen S. Sorin. New York Landmarks Conservancy, 1997. Hamilton Heights and its wider context in superbly researched walking tours.

*When Harlem Was in Vogue*, by David Levering Lewis. Knopf, 1981. An outstanding work of cultural history about African-American Harlem in the bloom of its youth.

# General Bibliography

*AIA Guide to New York City*, by Norval White and Elliot Willensky, Three Rivers Press, Fourth edition, 2000. Capsule summaries of significant buildings in all five boroughs with pithy commentary and thumbnail photographs. This useful compendium, identifying structures by architect, location, date, and style, has been the ultimate guide to New York's buildings since it was first published in 1967.

*An Architectural Guidebook to Brooklyn*, by Francis Morrone, Gibbs Smith, Publisher, 2001. Brooklyn was extensively developed in the nineteenth century when it was a separate city; the accessible and intelligent text focuses on northern and central Brooklyn and details the borough's many architectural treasures.

*The Architectural Guidebook to New York City*, by Francis Morrone, Gibbs Smith, Revised, 2002. How to look, where to look, and what to know about historic and contemporary buildings throughout Manhattan, coupled with discerning commentary.

*The Encyclopedia of New York City*, edited by Kenneth T. Jackson, The New-York Historical Society and Yale University Press, 1995. Second edition, 2008. An outstanding, comprehensive reference work with 4,288 entries on the history, people, and culture of New York; an indispensable resource for students and scholars.

*Gotham: A History of New York City to 1898*, by Edwin G. Burrows and Mike Wallace, Oxford University Press, 1999. A fact-laden, massive, and readable book by history professors from the City University of New York, who spent more than twenty years chronicling the city's cultural, economic, political, and physical development.

*Guide to New York City Landmarks*, New York City Landmarks Preservation Commission, edited by Matthew A. Postal, text by Andrew S. Dolkart and Matthew A. Postal, John Wiley & Sons, Fourth edition, 2009. This authoritative book provides straightforward descriptions of more than 1,200 individual landmarks and 90 historic districts designated by the NYC Landmarks Preservation Commission since it began in 1965. Short essays, "Of Special Interest," by Matthew A. Postal, group landmarks by thematic interest: artists, housing, modernism, transit, recent additions to historic districts, and more.

*Public Art New York*, by Jean Parker Phifer, W.W. Norton, 2009. From outdoor sculpture in public plazas and landscapes to murals and works of art in lobbies accessible to the public, organized by neighborhood, with maps suitable for a walking guide, this colorful volume focuses on how exemplary works of public art enrich urban public space.

*Preserving New York—Winning the Right to Protect a City's Landmarks*, by Anthony C. Wood, Routledge, 2008. The definitive book on the history of the preservation movement in New York City, including the pivotal role of the Municipal Art Society; clearly written and well researched, with exceptional photographic documentation.

*Shaping the City: New York and the Municipal Art Society*, by Gregory F. Gilmartin, Clarkson Potter, 1995. The issues and the battles are laid out here to show how the Municipal Art Society, a private organization founded in 1893 to beautify the city through public art, has become a civic powerhouse affecting growth and development in New York.

The five books listed below constitute a monumental series of documentary studies on New York City architecture and urbanism, extensively researched and illustrated, by Robert A. M. Stern, dean of the Yale School of Architecture, and principal partner, Robert A. M. Stern Architects, with prominent authors and architectural historians. They are:

*New York 1880: Architecture and Urbanism in the Gilded Age*, by Robert A. M. Stern, Thomas Mellins, and David Fishman, Monacelli, 1999.

*New York 1900: Metropolitan Architecture and Urbanism, 1890–1915*, by Robert A. M. Stern, Gregory F. Gilmartin, and John Massengale, Rizzoli, 1992.

*New York 1930: Architecture Between the Two World Wars*, by Robert A. M. Stern, Gregory Gilmartin, and Thomas Mellins, Rizzoli, 1994.

*New York 1960: Architecture and Urbanism Between the Second World War and the Bicentennial*, by Robert A. M. Stern, Thomas Mellins, and David Fishman, Monacelli, Second edition, 1997.

*New York 2000: Architecture and Urbanism from the Bicentennial to the Millennium*, by Robert A. M. Stern, David Fishman, and Jacob Tilove, Monacelli, 2006.

# About the Contributors

**KENT L. BARWICK**, president emeritus of The Municipal Art Society of New York, has been a leader of many urban campaigns, including the battle to save Grand Central Terminal and the creation of the Landmarks Law. He is the founder of the Preservation League of New York State, the New York Landmarks Conservancy, and the Historic Districts Council. He has played an active role in the Municipal Art Society's Imagine New York and Tribute in Light projects, which arose as a result of the 9/11 tragedy.

**TAMARA COOMBS**, director of programs and tours, has degrees in architecture and in writing about architecture and design. Before coming to MAS, she worked in preservation and the arts and led urban and rural study tours.

**ROBIN LYNN**, a native New Yorker, directed the MAS tour program for more than twelve years. She led MAS tours of New York's neighborhoods and studied architectural history at Columbia University. She coauthored *A Walking Tour of Cast Iron Architecture in SoHo* with Margot Gayle.

**FRANCIS MORRONE** is an art and architecture critic who wrote the weekly column "Abroad in New York" for the *New York Sun*. He writes book reviews, film criticism, and design criticism for many publications. He has written six books, including the acclaimed *An Architectural Guidebook to Brooklyn*. He lectures widely, teaches occasionally, and works on exhibitions.

**JUAN CAMILO OSORIO**, who produced the maps, is the MAS Planning Center senior geographic information systems (GIS) analyst and planner. He holds an MS in regional planning from the University of Massachusetts, Amherst, and a BA in architecture from the National University of Colombia, Bogotá.

**MATTHEW A. POSTAL** is an architectural historian specializing in twentieth-century architecture and urbanism. He holds a PhD in art history from the Graduate Center of the City University of New York. He has been a member of the research staff of the New York Landmarks Preservation Commission since 1998 and is an adjunct professor of architectural history at the New York School of Interior Design and Lewis and Clark College. He is the coauthor of the *Guide to New York City Landmarks*.

**GENEVIEVE R. SHERMAN**, MAS issues coordinator, assisted with map production and walking routes. She holds a BA in urban studies from Barnard College, where she was the editor of the urban studies journal *Rhapsody in Blue*.

**ALLISON SILVER**, a long-time member of MAS, is the editor of the *Washington Independent* and a former editor at "The Week in Review" of the *New York Times*.

**EDWARD A. TORAN** studied architecture and art history, and worked as an interior architect for large corporations for more than thirty years. He has conducted research in work-space development, applied arts, and industrial design, and has written and lectured extensively on these topics. Experienced in graphic and exhibition design, he brings a long-standing interest in photography as a communications tool and his skills as a computer programmer to his many, and varied, projects.

# Index

Page numbers in *italics* refer to illustrations

WITHDRAWN